THE DIARIES OF DAVID EPP
1837-1843

The Diaries of David Epp
1837-1843

Translated and Edited
by John B. Toews

Regent College Publishing
Vancouver, British Columbia

The Diaries of David Epp 1837-1843

First printing 2000 by Regent College Publishing,
an imprint of the Regent College Bookstore,
5800 University Boulevard, Vancouver, B.C. Canada V6T 2E4

The author and publisher wish to thank
William Schroeder for permission to reproduce
images on pages 8 and 192.

Printed on demand in the United States of America
The paper used in this publication meets the minimum
requirements of the American National Standard for Information
Sciences—Permanence of Paper for Printed Library Materials,
ANSI Z39.48-1984.

Canadian Cataloguing in Publication Data

Epp, David, 1781-1843
The diaries of David Epp

Includes bibliographical references.
ISBN 0-88865-440-5 (Can)
ISBN 1-57383-157-3 (U.S.)

1. Epp, David, 1781-1843—Diaries. 2. Mennonites—Russia—Diaries. 3.
Mennonites—Russia—History. I. Toews, John B., 1934-
II. Title

BX8143.E76A3 2000 289.7'47'092 C99-911141-8

to those forebears who faithfully lived the Gospel in bygone eras

Contents

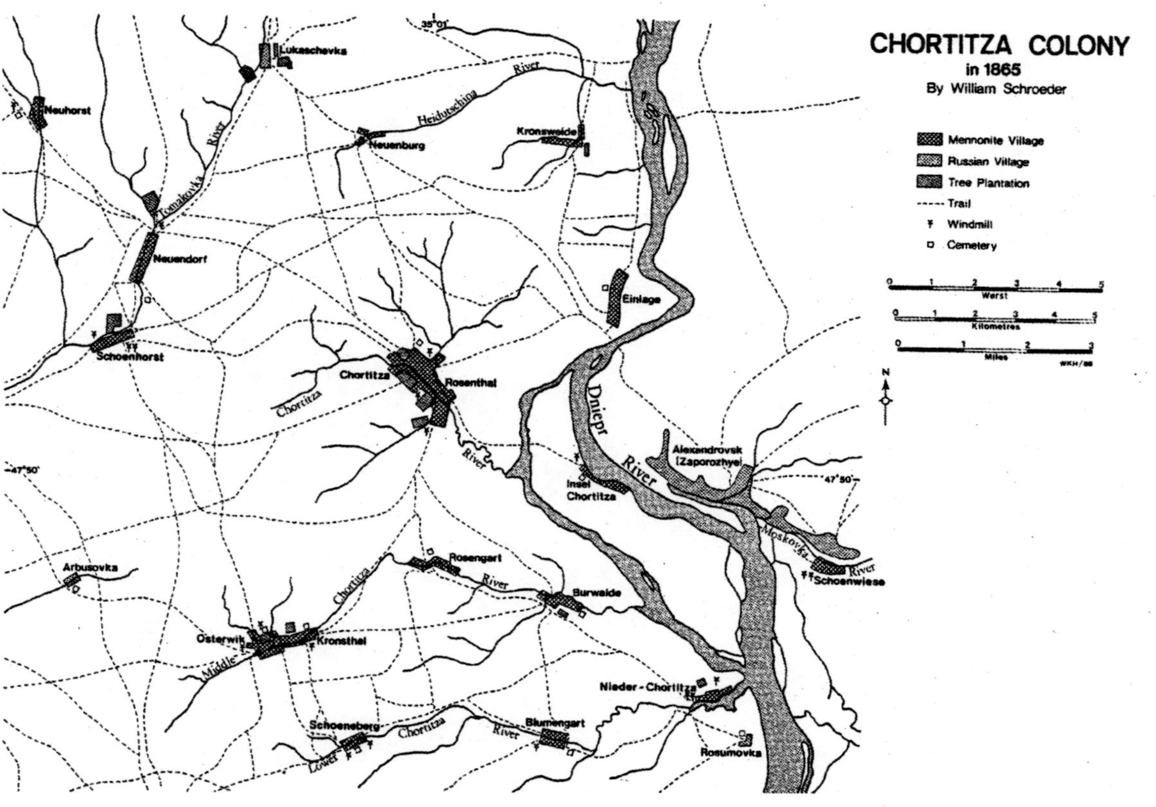
CHORTITZA COLONY
in 1865
By William Schroeder
Mennonite Village
Russian Village
Tree Plantation
Trail
Windmill
Cemetery
Werst
Kilometres
Miles
N
35°01'
47°50'
Lukaschevka
Neuhorst
Neuenburg
Heidutschina River
Kronsweide
Tomakovka River
Neuendorf
Einlage
Schoenhorst
Chortitza
Rosenthal
Dniepr River
Alexandrovsk (Zaporozhye)
Insel Chortitza
Moskovka River
Schoenwiese
Arbusovka
Rosengart
Burwalde
Osterwik
Kronsthal
Middle Chortitza River
Nieder-Chortitza
Schoeneberg
Blumengart
Lower Chortitza River
Rosumovka

Foreword

Diaries allow us to follow another person's pathway even though it is long removed from our own. In the case of the Chortitza minister David Epp we can walk alongside him from 1837 until his death in 1843. His was an era in which the horse was still the main source of power for transport and agriculture, where the germ theory of disease was unknown, and where custom and tradition governed most facets of religious and civil life.

Reading the varied entries, we sense what was important and dear to Epp personally. His primary focus is the life of the church and its impact on the community. A deeply spiritual man, he is burdened by the moral and lifestyle lapses of his fellow Christians. For him relationships within the community matter more than anything else. Ironically his farming activities, which nourished and sustained him, are rarely mentioned. Life in the community meant dealing with the foibles of human nature and Epp does not hesitate to express his impatience with the stupidities committed by some of his fellow Mennonites. Yet there is a sustaining optimism amid his many moments of frustration and despair: the hope that the Gospel can bring betterment and restoration.

I would like to thank the Mennonite Heritage Centre in Winnipeg for making the material available to me, and the senior members of the various Epp clans for allowing me to publish this diary of their pious forebear. It will hopefully provide some hours of pleasure for the ordinary reader who has an interest in the Russian Mennonite story.

I would also like to thank William J.J. Riediger for his generous support in this publication endeavour.

On occasion words in the diaries could not be deciphered, and in some instances the biblical texts cited were in error. In such cases a question mark is used.

John B. Toews
July 1999

Introduction

Early Settlement

In David Epp's Chortitza the west bank of the Dnieper river was, with some exceptions, rather high and steep. The streams and rivers draining the landscape ran swiftly and over the centuries had created an undulating landscape of hills and valleys. Floods caused by sudden thundershowers or rapidly melting snow often eroded rather than enriched the land. Farming conditions stood in stark contrast to the floodplains of the Vistula Delta which the settlers left some four decades earlier. Chortitza, with its sandy and often poor soil, was a settlement site more suited to raising cattle and sheep than grain. Even this endeavour was complicated by sporadic rainfall or more occasionally, severe drought. Then there were the extremes of a continental climate with the hot, dry winds of summer and the icy blasts of arctic air in winter. There was a small consolation for David Epp and his co-religionists. The early colonists had settled along the larger streams which drained the region. Living in a valley often meant not seeing the neighbouring village, but it also meant the comfort of the sheltering hills surrounding them.

The sense of the romantic, which even today characterizes the Chortitza villages, belied the hardships characterizing the early years of settlement. Loans and building supplies promised by the Russian government were slow in coming. Then too the settlers were inexperienced in matters of self-government. It must have been extremely difficult to manage village and district affairs in a new country on the one hand and simultaneously deal with capricious Russian officials on the other. Furthermore, the first settlers had no ministers to provide spiritual structure for their lives by presiding over worship services, marriages, baptisms or burials. The struggle to survive by farming in the alien land probably eclipsed all other difficulties. Attempts to raise oats, barley, buckwheat and winter wheat met with poor success. Lentils, millet and winter rye produced marginal harvests. Livestock and horses brought from Prussia often succumbed to severe winter cold, starvation and disease, or were stolen by covetous neighbours.

The year 1800 marked a turning point in the viability of the Chortitza colony. Additional migrants from Prussia steadily augmented livestock herds, farm inventory and the amount of money in circulation. Loans, long overdue, were finally made available. The most crucial event ensuring the eventual success of the settlement related to the appointment of Samuel Contenius as head of the newly created Office of Guardianship for Foreign Settlers in New Russia. The role of the Commission was to deal with the difficulties experienced by all foreign settlers in New Russia—Germans, Swedes, Rumanians, Greeks, Bulgarians and Mennonites. Contenius soon addressed the economic and administrative chaos plaguing the foreign settlements in New Russia. Destitute Chortitza felt his strong, guiding hand in several areas. He stressed the planting of trees and gardens in the villages as well as the establishment of forests. In 1802 Contenius wrote a letter to elder Cornelius Warkentin in Rosenort near Elbing in Prussia that reflected his strategy. He outlined a twofold approach to cope with the sandy soil and inadequate rainfall of the Chortitza colony. He stressed that Merino sheep (of Spanish extraction) as well as horses and cattle might thrive on the native grasses covering the valleys and hills of the region. Furthermore, economic diversification involving cottage industries utilizing readily available raw materials could supplement the settlers' income and eventually lead to the birth of milling and industry in the region.

The letter suggests that Contenius took a special interest in attracting more Mennonite settlers from Prussia. He not only persuaded the governor to reserve some of the best settlement lands for them but also secured a promised loan of 1,300 rubles per family compared with some 300 to 500 rubles for settlers of other nationalities. Then there was advice on possible travel routes, house building styles and on "how best the Mennonites can prosper in this region." The letter contained additional information. The Chortitza region had been enlarged by some 14,000 acres; cattle and sheep production expanded; and experiments were being conducted in fruit production and wine making.

The good will of Russia's rulers toward the Mennonite settlers continued into the 1840s. Important state visitors arrived in the colonies with some regularity. David Epp records the visit of the reform-minded minister of state domains, Count P. Kiselev and his reception by the leaders of the settlement on August 6, 1841. The minister spoke only Russian, the Mennonites only German. Fortunately the district secretary G. Penner was able to serve as translator. Some two months later (October 2, 1841) the Grand Duchess Elena Pavlovna and her daughter Maria Michaelovna made a brief stopover at Einlage. The teacher Heinrich Heese was quick to acquaint the illustrious visitor with plans for the new secondary school. It was completed by the end of 1841 but as Epp complained: "Who is to pay for the cost of the building—the congregation or the general treasury?" (December 31, 1841).

Epp's diary makes frequent reference to the Chortitza community sheep farm. It was founded in 1803 on some 3,040 dessiatine of land generally unsuitable for cultivation. The government, thanks to Contenius's influence, donated the first thirty Merino sheep to the project. A severe winter in 1812-13 devastated the flock, yet by 1819 the colony again possessed more than 1,000 sheep. In the days when Epp was penning his diary the Chortitza settlement possessed more sheep per farm than the wealthier and larger Molotschna settlement.

Early Chortitza was well supplied with craftsmen. The first emigration lists help explain the situation—craftsmen were far more numerous than farmers. Thirty years after settlement a sizeable assortment of weavers, tailors, shoemakers and carpenters still served the community, not to mention cask and barrel makers, joiners and lathe experts. The presence of at least sixteen blacksmiths reflected not only the demand for better farm implements but also the switch from wooden to iron axels on farm wagons. In David Epp's day locally manufactured wagons began to make their first appearance.

The first flour mill powered by water was built by the Chortitza settlement in the 1790s and functioned for some ten years. By 1805 a horse or treadmill was built in Yekaterinoslav by a Heinrich Thiessen whose family milling business would continue to function for more than a century. In Chortitza itself the first windmill was erected around 1830. David Epp might have obtained his flour from either type of mill.

Even in Epp's day Chortitza farmers still faced one insurmountable problem—the lack of markets for farm produce. While cities like Yekaterinoslav and Alexandrovsk lay within easy driving distance, they were not large enough to absorb the excess production. Dnieper river transport was still in its infancy though some grain trade was possible in Cherson and Nikolajev. These cities also provided a limited market for butter, cheese, as well as mutton and beef. For Chortitza distant markets only became available in 1863 when regularized ship transport was established from Alexandrovsk down the Dnieper to Odessa.

Schools

The first teacher of significance in the Chortitza Colony was David Hausknecht, a Swiss national, whose family migrated to West Prussia, joined the Mennonites, and eventually migrated to Chortitza in 1828. Here he taught in the Einlage village school for ten years, then founded a private secondary school in Einlage. Once in Einlage, he appears to have established cultural and intellectual links with Europe which apparently brought some educational and devotional materials to the Chortitza Colony. It remains uncertain how this literature impacted David Epp. One source suggests he engaged in considerable self-study and outside reading. His diaries, which survive from 1837 nowhere reflect such an interest, but that does not mean that the Hausknecht material could not have been formative in his younger days. The same source also reports that Epp gathered a reading group together which included a local carpenter, the district secretary, a local businessperson and David Hausknecht.

One of the earliest accounts of the Mennonite secondary school in Russia involves the career of one Tobia Voth (1791—?) He was trained as a teacher in Russia and held his first teaching positions there. He was the first teacher in a secondary school organized by Orlov villagers in the Molotschna. The school's avowed object was to provide a place for the spread of Christian teaching and to raise the standard of High German. Voth came to the school in 1822 and resigned under pressure from Johann Cornies, the Mennonite landowner and entrepreneur, in

1829. In Voth's place Cornies appointed Heinrich Heese, a person he felt would teach with greater "manliness" than his predecessor. Heese taught in the Ohrloff school from 1829 to 1842.

Heinrich Heese, born into a Lutheran family in Prussia, migrated to Russia in 1808. He must have joined the Mennonite Church in Chortitza out of conviction and possibly also to marry Katharina Penner. In 1812 he became district secretary and moved to Chortitza. His sojourn at the Ohrloff school ended when he came into conflict with Johann Cornies. David Epp records his transfer to Chortitza in 1842, where he became the first teacher in the newly founded secondary school. Epp did not live to witness his dismissal from this second teaching position by Cornies in 1846. According to Epp's diary entries, Heese became an acceptable candidate for the Chortitza secondary school position in April,1841. He arrived in the settlement on June 21 and the very next day visited Epp already campaigning on behalf of the new school. At the end of the year Epp somewhat prosaically reported: "A *Zentralschule* has been built thanks to the insistence of the teacher Heinrich Heese"(Dec. 31, 1841). David Epp was a very active participant in the establishment of the school. He was present at Heese's installation (May 27), helped to establish suitable quarters for the school (June 21) and participated in the drafting of its statutes (July 7).

The Epp diaries also make reference to the private school established on Peter Schmidt's estate at Steinbach. Epp first visited this school in mid-September, 1838, during a trip to the Molotschna. In January, 1839, he reports that he "left Heinrich with the teachers Lange and Friesen so that he can learn German and Russian—Each day there will be four hours of instruction in German and four hours of instruction in Russian." Heinrich returned to Chortitza on April 20. The diaries do not indicate whether he ever returned to Steinbach but we do know that Heinrich later became the head teacher at the Chortitza secondary school. Friedrich Lange was a nephew of Wilhelm Lange who accompanied his Old Flemish congregation in their migration from Brandenburg, Prussia to Gnadenfeld, Molotschna in 1834. Friedrich himself arrived in 1837. If the diary entry of May 18, 1840 is any indication, there was ongoing contact between Lange, Schmidt and Epp.

David Epp's diaries assume that elementary education was well entrenched in both the Chortitza and Molotschna colonies. It is difficult to establish the precise qualifications of the village school teacher, though it is reasonable to assume that by 1837 the secondary school in Ohrloff would have produced some teachers for the Chortitza settlement as would Hauskrecht's Einlage private school. A high percentage of village children, male and female, attended school. The schools normally functioned from October to April, coinciding with the rhythm of the agricultural year. Our knowledge of the elementary school curriculum is sketchy though we may safely assume the presence of such subjects as reading, writing and arithmetic. Judging by the quality and penmanship of Mennonite letters reaching government offices in St. Petersburg the literacy level was substantial.

Locally the level of education often depended on the dynamic operative between the local village and its teacher. If the diary account of Heinrich Heese's employment is normative a negotiated contract was the order of the day. In addition to a salary the village might grant free board and room to the single teacher or even provide a house if the teacher was married and had a family. Furthermore the village may offer a supply of hay for livestock, access to pasture, an allowance of grain and/or flour as well as a garden plot. If a village was progressively minded and concerned with the welfare of its children the teacher's lot and livelihood was tolerable. In such a setting the teacher became an agent for cultural advancement. Negative dispositions on the part of the village or its teacher naturally produced the opposite result. If a village possessed concerned and influential leaders like David Epp, a good education for the children was assured.

Birth, Disease and Death

Epp the minister and farmer reflects the pragmatism of one who was steadily in contact with birth, disease and death. Here was a Christian realism buttressed by the hope of resurrection on one hand and the acceptance of the reality of suffering and death on the other. Professional medical services were simply not available, though late in November,1837, a Dr. von Grosheim set up a practice in Neuenberg. Epp wondered if the Mennonite settlers would know "how to appreciate a doctor" (Nov. 23, 1837).

For Epp personally most diseases were not readily identifiable. Usually he will speak of an illness (*Krankheit*) in the most general terms, though on occasion he will specify dropsy, small pox, apoplexy, intestinal inflammation and dysentery. At times he simply refers to a fever resulting in death. Even if he identifies an illness, Epp knows little of home remedies. He possesses no knowledge of preventive medicine, especially in relation to communicable diseases or infections. There is no understanding as to the origins of disease for the world of that day had not yet discovered its viral or bacterial cause. Quarantine or isolation was unheard of and so the community stood helpless in the face of typhoid, cholera, diphtheria, whooping cough or measles epidemics. The sequential death of young children in the same family were especially heart breaking. Again and again Epp stood at the grave site of a newborn, a pre-school child, a ten-year-old or even teenager. If the reader finds his funeral texts repetitive it would be well to remember the many little children whose souls he commended to God and whose bodies he committed to the earth.

The presence of the folk healer or local hope-giver cannot be detected in David Epp's diary. Two decades later (1860s) his son Jacob identifies the local midwife, bonesetter, herbalist, tooth puller and even blood-letter in his detailed and extensive diary. Except for Dr. Grosheim his father was apparently not aware of these healers or simply failed to mention them.

Though Epp documented his funeral services in a terse abbreviated fashion, he nevertheless provides us with important information. Where possible he identifies the nature of the illness as well as the cause and time of death. He records the precise age of the individual, the length of a marriage or sequential marriages and the number of children and grandchildren from each union (predeceased and surviving). In doing so he provides sobering statistics on child morality and adult life expectancy.

Medically one marvels at David Epp's acceptance of the "order of things." Nowhere in his diary is the sense of uncontrollable grief or panic in the face of disease and death. His funeral texts affirm resurrection and future life. Dying also occurred in the context of community. Family, friends and ministers were usually present throughout the process. A person died at home. It was here that the body was washed, prepared for burial and kept until the funeral. Here was a normal, deeply realistic grieving process. Family and community stood together in death and burial and did not disperse to distant places a few hours after the funeral.

David Epp's Religious World

On New Year's day, 1837, David Epp tersely recorded that Chortitza Mennonites had gathered in Schoenhorst, Chortitza, Neu-Osterwick and Neuendorf for worship. On this day, as in previous years, those assembled heard words of comfort and admonishment. By now the settlement had enjoyed stability for almost half a century and assured a reasonable comfort level for the descendants of the original pioneers. New Russia was home and the customary liturgical practices associated with the ecclesiastical year provided a sense that all was well. The celebration of the New Year meant at least two days of services. Another service followed on the Feast of Epiphany (January 6). The celebration of Easter and Pentecost highlighted the ecclesiastical year. Special services were held on Palm Sunday, Good Friday as well as Easter Sunday and Monday. Christmas, a three-day festival, meant two days with formal worship services.

Amid all the festivities another crucial rite, baptism, was in various stages of preparation. The weekly instruction of young adults usually coincided with the Sunday morning reading of the confession of faith. Six Sundays, each one devoted to reading half the articles of faith, ensured a minimum level of theological literacy among members of the congregation. By the third or fourth reading of the articles the baptismal candidates formally presented themselves. On the fifth Sunday the *Bruederschaft* (the male members of the local congregation) officially voted to approve the candidates. On the last Sunday before baptism these young adults sat on the front bench and listened as the confession of faith was read for the sixth time. They were then questioned by the elder as to their faith and responded affirmatively. Baptism was administered on the following Sunday. Since communion was scheduled a week later, the newly baptised young people heard the customary *Vorbereitungspredigt* (preparatory sermon). The Sunday following the celebration of the Lord's Supper the presiding minister or elder preached a *Dankpredigt* (a sermon of thanks and praise).

The rite of baptism was probably the yearly highpoint for the inhabitants of the Chortitza colony. Its value as a tool for spiritual renewal and instruction was obvious. For the young the memorization of the catechism fixed the fundamentals of faith in their minds. Mature Christians benefitted by once more hearing the articles of faith read and listening to the young people speak their pledges of faith and commitment. The sound of water being poured on the heads of baptismal candidates symbolized the continuity of faith and community. A traditional liturgy affirmed new spiritual life as another generation joined the church—that was comforting.

Chortitza Mennonites felt themselves to be different and apart from the rest of society. After all they belonged to a dissenting group that insisted that the church was voluntary in membership, that it was separate from the state and that peace was always preferable to war. Settlement in New Russia brought all these freedoms. In David Epp's world most Mennonites were serious about applying faith to the affairs of everyday life. They knew what private and public morality demanded and what a circumspect lifestyle meant. The life of Christ was regarded as a model for living and the Sermon on the Mount as a norm for lifestyle issues. As these concerns spanned the decades they moulded a society that fused religion and custom and in which the interests of church and society were thoroughly intermingled.

Diary writer Epp was comfortable with the arrangement. At one point in his life he had been elected a *Lehrer* (teacher/minister), a lifelong position provided there was no ethical or moral lapse. In addition to his regular preaching duties he belonged to the *Lehrdienst* (ministerial council), whose individual members might be referred to as *der Ehrsame* (the honorable one) or simply *Ohm*, a designation implying respect and seniority. The jurisdiction of the *Lehrdienst* was wide ranging. It included almost every kind of civil infraction or an occasional criminal one. Theft, dishonesty, drunkenness, assault, adultery, deviant sexuality, disputes of every kind—all such cases came before the *Lehrdienst*. If the issue could not be resolved at this level it was passed on to the *Bruederschaft* for further debate and discussion. There was no appeal from its decision. In the event of noncompliance the individual was excommunicated from the congregation, which meant not only acute embarrassment but the potential loss of legal privileges associated with belonging to the larger Mennonite community. Both the *Lehrdienst* and *Bruederschaft*, as Epp's diaries repeatedly illustrate, were powerful tools in regulating the life of the Chortitza community.

David Epp the pastor records two overriding concerns in his diary: deviant sexuality and drunkenness. He is candid in delineating what is acceptable sexual conduct. Sexual activity occurred only within marriage. Adultery while married and pre-marital sex were serious offences in the eyes of the community as a whole. Invariably when offences were discovered or confessed it was a matter for both the *Lehrdienst* and *Bruderschaft*. The offending parties were routinely excommunicated and readmitted some weeks later if contrition and repentance were evident. Cases of incest, rape and sodomy deeply impacted Epp. Especially shocking was the exposure of a newborn child by its young mother and the case of an infant fathered by a Russian lad, whose Mennonite mother then joined the Orthodox church.

Instances of alcohol abuse are frequently cited in Epp's diaries. The village pub, usually a small business operated out of a home, was frequently the scene of intoxication and fighting. Similarly Russian villages or district fairs offered a ready supply of liquor. Adolescent youth, perhaps viewing alcohol as a rite of passage, appeared before the *Lehrdienst* in surprisingly large numbers. Public cursing, wife beating, fighting and even accidental death—Epp associates all such *Lehrdienst* matters with drunkenness. He especially laments the drinking and dancing associated with Mennonite wedding celebrations.

As a member of the *Lehrdienst* Epp encountered issues as varied as life itself. Orphaned children, a frequent reality in those days, needed new homes, contract disputes required arbitration and public mischief and juvenile delinquency demanded appropriate punishment. On other occasions the ministerial council presided over the enforcement of district and village bylaws, instances of petty theft, the construction of two new churches as well as church and welfare levies. It also hired the first new doctor for the Chortitza region and made the decision to establish a secondary school, employing its first teacher, Heinrich Heese. Perhaps it was little wonder that Epp is somewhat brooding and pessimistic in his diaries—as a member of the *Lehrdienst* he encountered only the problems prevalent in his community and failed to hear its joy and laughter.

There was possibly another reason for Epp's despondency—the nature of his spirituality. He was a deeply pious and utterly sincere Christian pilgrim. Epp upheld the role of God's grace in salvation. His sermon texts consistently stress the need for repentance, the centrality of Christ and the need for faith. He constantly stresses the importance of spiritual rebirth and inner transformation, but does not explain the nature of that process. The diaries make frequent reference to *Busse* (repentance) and *Bekehrung* (conversion), but nowhere does Epp explain whether this was a gradual, protracted affirmation of faith or a sudden climax bringing with it an overwhelming assurance of salvation. His sermons nevertheless assumed that his listeners were believers, deeply conscious of the fact that in Christ their sins were forgiven. Yet, if the diary portrait is correct, Epp's struggle for salvation assurance is ongoing and at times agonizing.

The diary reader may be troubled by Epp's moments of spiritual despair, his lack of joy and his hesitancy to celebrate his salvation. In the words of the apostle Paul, he appears to work out his salvation with "fear and trembling." Why the reluctance to speak of liberating faith, the ecstasy of conversion or the day-to-day happiness of Christ's indwelling presence? While Epp stressed faith he also believed that the Gospel needed expression in everyday life. Mennonites had always held that the church must be the salt of the earth by seeking to imitate Christ's lifestyle. The life of the church needed to reflect the nature of God's kingdom. Goodness and godliness must express itself within the Christian community. One stood before God together with one's sister and brother, never alone. Yet the attempt to mirror God's kingdom was beset by human frailties. There were quarrels and divisions within the community as there were spiritual and moral shipwrecks. Such failings had to be addressed in love by the *Lehrdienst* and *Bruederschaft*. Perhaps Epp's spiritual despondency was rooted in the fact that he saw only the sinners who appeared before the *Lehrdienst*, whose offences represented a small minority within the community. The goodness of the majority was overlooked. A closely related issue probably augmented his pessimism. It was assumed that all adults in the colony belonged to the church. Certainly the notion of a free church based on voluntary membership constituted the ideal, but in reality Epp's church embraced all of Mennonite society. In such a setting the struggle for goodness was unending.

David Epp's religious world is an expanding one. He makes frequent visits to the Molotschna and receives guests from there in return. There are relatives and visitors from the Mennonite churches in Prussia. Epp records the visit of the British Bible Society representative John Melville who persuaded Epp to accept "six boxes of Bibles and New Testaments for sale and distribution" (July 22, 1842). It is possible that Melville and similar visitors expanded the circulation of devotional and expository literature, some of which reflected the concerns of German pietism with its emphasis on personal faith and rigorous discipleship. It is perhaps not surprising to find that mid-century religious revival in Chortitza began when a young man began to read the writings of the German pietist Ludwig Hofacker (1798-1828). Mennonite dissenters of the 1860s were likewise reading other evangelical literature from Germany.

Thanks to his frequent visits to the Molotschna settlement, David Epp kept abreast of the ecclesiastical politics in that region. His September 20, 1838, reference to elders Fast, Warkentin and Wedel reflected a complex accumulation of issues. The colonization of the Molotschna settlement, beginning in 1804, brought a mix of migrants from Danzig and West Prussia. These were rooted in both the Flemish and Frisian traditions. By the early nineteenth century, the customs and traditions that separated Mennonites in Prussia had begun to blur. This was not the case in Russia. In 1817 the Flemish congregation in Ohrloff, Molotschna elected Jacob Fast as their elder, though not without some opposition. When he died in 1820 another elder, Bernhard Fast, was elected. As a progressive leader Fast promoted higher education and co-operated with the Russian Bible Society in order to distribute Bibles both in and beyond the Molotschna. A revolt within his congregation led by the ultra conservative Jacob Warkentin left Fast with only one quarter of his congregation.

Now it was Warkentin's turn to lose his congregation. His situation was complicated by the fact that the delicate balance between the Mennonite state and the church increasingly weighed in favour of the state. The wealthy estate owner and agricultural businessman Johann Cornies had gained control of the South Russian Agricultural Union, first founded in Odessa in 1828. Cornies was appointed as the permanent head of the agency by the Guardian's Committee. While the Union's farming objectives were commendable, its dictatorial methods clashed with Mennonite egalitarianism. Even worse was its intrusion into congregational life and practice.

Tensions came to a head when a young member of Warkentin's congregation, Johann Regier, was elected as district mayor. An effective administrator, he was nevertheless a confirmed alcoholic. When congregational discipline proved ineffective, Warkentin complained to Inzov, the head of the Guardian's Committee in 1838. Nothing was done and Regier was elected to a third term of office. In 1841 a Peter

Toews replaced Regier as district mayor but his election was not honoured by Johann Cornies. Warkentin appealed to the *Comitaet* (Guardian's Committee) which upheld Toews's election but under the circumstances felt a new election to be appropriate. Regier died before it could be held. The new head of the Guardian's Committee, von Hahn, now accused Warkentin of interfering in civil matters. Ignoring the congregation's autonomy as well as the settlers' right to the religious freedom guaranteed by the *Privilegium*, Hahn divided the congregation regionally. Dirk Warkentin was appointed to the Petershagen-Lichtenau church in the western Molotschna, Heinrich Toews to the Pordenau church and Heinrich Wiens to the Margenau-Schoensee church. None of the three were elders at the time of their appointment. Another elder, Peter Schmidt, ordained Wiens, who in turn ordained the other two candidates. Little wonder that David Epp commented: "The district office and the Agricultural Society rule more through despotism than through gentleness as Jesus taught" (December 29, 1840). By 1842 he cryptically reported: "Elder Jacob Warkentin of Altonau has been stripped of his office" (December 27). Epp did not live to see the ongoing struggle which soon deprived elder Heinrich Wiens of his office.

In the Chortitza religious world David Epp primarily interacted with elder Jacob Dyck of Rosenthal. Dyck died in 1854 at the age of seventy-six. He had been a minister for six years, then elected as elder, a position he held for forty-two years. Judging from his diary entries Epp found Dyck too accommodating of his congregation's failings and too ready to readmit excommunicated sinners back into the fold. The diary comments suggest that Dyck did not share Epp's moral earnestness and participated in unnecessary ecclesiastical politics. A few weeks before his death Epp wrote: "Spiritually we have reached a new low, especially in our ecclesiastical leadership" (March 28, 1843). Some years earlier he had observed: "It's so sad when premature judgment, hate, partisan politics and ignorance rule" (December 26, 1838). Just over a month later he again laments: "As long as there is no inner renewal there will be no peace in our society" (February 2, 1839). Epp's pastoral duties and concerns find expression in the diaries until April 23, 1843. It was his last entry. He died as a result of a stroke on May 15. The diaries conclude with the words: "Faith, love and hope, these three [remain]." It seems fitting to believe that these words inwardly sustained him during his thirty-seven years of public ministry.

Two other jurisdictions are occasionally mentioned in Epp's diaries. Elder Jacob Dyck frequently interacted with elder Jakob Hildebrandt of the nearby "Kronsweide church." Early Frisian migrants had settled in the villages of Einlage, Kronsweide, Insel Khortitza as well as Schoenwiese and Kronsgarten. Inhabitants of these villages could of course choose to belong to elder Dyck's parish if they so desired. The second ecclesiastical jurisdiction mentioned by Epp is Bergthal, a Chortitza daughter colony begun in 1836. The diaries suggest frequent clerical and fraternal visits between the two colonies.

David Epp often mentions the names of his fellow ministers—Jacob Penner, H. Penner, Jacob Regier, Johann Penner and Johann Dyck. On April 16, 1840, he reports the election of two new ministers Heinrich Penner and David Wiens. On the following Sunday both "sat in their designated places." The working relationship between the ministers appears to have been a harmonious one. Epp is not afraid to criticize his elder, but nowhere does he make any negative statement with regard to his fellow workers.

Epp cites his preaching texts with great regularity. They are broad ranging and reflect relatively little repetition. Unfortunately he cites only his text and not the theme he emphasized. There is more text repetition in his funeral sermons, an understandable practice if in some years you preach almost as many funeral as public worship sermons. In an average year Epp might be expected to preach up to fifty sermons. Unfortunately no sermon outlines have survived.

An interesting item in the diary involves Epp's record of communion attendance in both Chortitza and Neuendorf. Weather conditions obviously played a role. Services held in February were more sparsely attended than those held in June. In 1839 for example, 186 participated in the Chortitza communion held on February 5. By contrast, 478 people attended the service held on May 28. In 1840, 170 people attended the February communion service while 511 were present during the June celebration. Many of Epp's co-religionists only celebrated communion once a year. Little wonder that it was a service of special liturgical significance and preparation.

Family

The Epps of early nineteenth century Chortitza were not only destined to become one of the more prominent and influential families of

David Epp's Family

David Epp (1781-1843) ––––– Maria Wiens (1779-1815)

Barbara (1810-1891)
m. P. Rempel

David (1812-1855)

Maria (1815-1846)
m. B. Friesen J. Sawatzky

David Epp (1781-1843) ––––– Helena Thiessen (1797-1864)

Heinrich	Diedrich	Jacob	Johann	Helena	Heinrich	Johann	Anna	Abraham	Katharina
1816-24	1819-1900	1820-90	1822-25	1825-73	1827-96	1830-88	1833-1919	1836-60	1839-1915

that settlement, but also of the Mennonites in Russia. Diary writer Epp was the son of David Epp (1750-1802) and Anna Bergman (1762-1796) who were married on August 17, 1780. According to the genealogical records left by his son Jacob Epp (1820-1890), David first married Maria Wiens (1779-1815). On February 1, 1816, David Epp married a second time, to Helena Thiessen. The accompanying chart may help the reader identify the children from both marriages. The first marriage lasted twelve years and eight months. In all there were nine children born to this union, four sons and five daughters. Only one son and two daughters survived. David Epp's second marriage to Helena Thiessen produced ten children.

David Epp appears as an affectionate, caring father in the diaries, as is illustrated by his interest in Heinrich's education or his search for a bride for Jacob. He may also have been a caring husband, though the diaries make no special mention of his second wife. Helena was much younger than David and continued to bear children as late as 1839, just four years before her husband's death. Her role as wife, mother and housekeeper is assumed but never directly acknowledged. The large family was possibly beset by indebtedness and poverty. Not long after David Epp's death the farm in Chortitza was sold and his widow with her five dependent children moved into a small cottage in the village. Except for visits to the sheep farm or a wool-marketing journey to Kharkov, David Epp never mentioned the fact that he and his family depended on the land for his livelihood. He does review the grain and cattle prices at the end of each year but the reader of the diaries comes away with the impression that David's interests lay elsewhere—in the realm of the spiritual.

1837

January 1

James 1:5 "If any of you lacks wisdom he should ask God, who gives generously to all without finding fault and it will be given to him." On Friday, New Year's, I preached in Chortitza on the text ? Elder J. Dyck preached in Schoenhorst; J. Regier in Neu-Osterwick; Peter Dyck in Neuendorf. O Holy Spirit, give us strength to put off the old self and sin and "to put on the new self created to be like God in true righteousness and holiness" (Eph. 4:24).

January 3

The first Sunday [of the month]. I preached in Einlage on Matthew 11:28; H. Penner [preached] in Chortitza; J. Regier in Osterwick. O Holy Spirit, give me strength to leave the sin that still plagues and exhausts me and help me to follow your commands.

January 6

The feast of Epiphany. I preached in Schoenhorst on Matthew 2: 1-13; Regier [preached] in Chortitza; Peter Dyck in Osterwick. Oh Holy Spirit, you morning star, rise in all our hearts.

January 10

I preached in Chortitza on Psalm 39:6; H. Penner [preached] in Schoenhorst. Lord help me remember that I must die and leave here so that my life has a sense of direction.

A brotherhood meeting. The step-daughter of J. Thiessen of Schoeneberg has slept with a Lutheran lad and given birth to a child. She was excommunicated from the congregation.

January 17

I preached in Chortitza on Matthew 20:29. There were only eleven present on account of the minus 19° temperatures![1] One minister and two deacons were present but no elder. The worship service was held in the minister's room. Jacob Braun preached in Neu-Osterwick. May all of us, O Holy Jesus, be your true disciples.

January 18

I preached a funeral message on ? in the parental home in Schoenhorst. The son of Salmon Neufeld died on January 14, 2 PM after an eighteen-day illness. He was three years, seven months and nine days old. May our departure be like that of an innocent child.

January 24

I preached in Schoenhorst on Matthew 22:2-13; H. Penner [preached] in Chortitza. The congregation was informed that the preparatory sermon [for communion] will be given at three locations.[2] Holy Jesus, I dedicate myself to you body and soul.

A brotherhood meeting. The step-daughter of J. Thiessen of Schoenberg was readmitted into church by elder Jacob Dyck. Create in me, O Lord, a pure heart, Amen.

January 28

I presided at the wedding of Claas Wiebe and Helena Schellenberg at the Jacob Wiebe residence on Chortitza Island. May the Lord's blessing rest upon these newlyweds.

January 29

A [joint meeting of the ministerial council and district council] was held at the residence of elder J. Dyck in Rosenthal.

1. It was agreed that the head of the Orphan Administration, Aron Sudermann, will get an increase of fifty rubles per year because of his age. It will only apply to successors who also reach his age.

2. Abram Penner has not been accepted into the Russian Church because of his corrupt lifestyle. Since he is still circulating within the community, the District Office [*Gebietsamt*][3] asked him to appear before them in order to talk about his misdeeds and give him some good advice, which we hope he will follow.

3. Peter Reimer, a cottager [*Anwohner*][4] from Neu-Chortitza is likewise living among the Russians. He will be asked to return to the colony so that he can be dealt with.

4. We want to reply to Dr. von Grosheim's letter (1836) to me and ask him under what conditions he would be willing to open a [medical] practice here. I was assigned to write the letter.

5. It was decided that Jacob Braun from Schoeneberg, who is presently a teacher of the Bergthaler Settlement near Mariupol, be transferred here this coming spring. A petition will be sent to the *Comitaet* [a shortened form for the *Fuersorge Komitee* in Odessa][5] on his behalf.

6. A new edition of hymnals from Riga was authorized.

7. There was some discussion about brandy contracts and smuggled goods, but nothing was decided.

Those present were elder Jacob Dyck; the ministers [*Lehrer*] D. Epp, H. Penner, Jacob Penner, Jacob Braun; the deacons Peter Hildebrand and ? Dyck; the members of the district office Jacob Bandesch (?), and the landowners Jacob von Kampen and Isbrand Braun.

January 31

I preached in Neu-Osterwick on the text ? Elder Jacob Dyck [preached] the preparatory sermon in Chortitza; brother H. Penner in Schoenhorst. If you know, blessed are you if you obey.

February 1

I preached the funeral sermon on Hebrews 13:14 at the home of the painter Franz Voth. His son Franz, who was ill since birth, died at the age of ten weeks. Blessed are those who die in infancy for they die in the Lord.

February 7

Elder J. Dyck celebrated communion with 216 members present. His text was Isaiah 53: 5-6. I am like a straying, lost sheep. Saviour, seek out your servant.

February 14

Elder J. Dyck celebrated communion a second time with ? members present. He used the same text. The Lord is near to those who call upon him, earnestly call upon him.

February 21

I preached the sermon of thanks in Chortitza. My text was Ephesians 1:3. Brother H. Penner [preached] in Schoenhorst; J. Braun in Osterwick. Thanks, eternal thanks for your love, my Lord and my God.

Afternoon I presided at the wedding of the young man Peter Krause and the young lady Agata Dyck at the Abraham Dyck residence in Einlage. The Lord bless them and keep them.

February 28

I preached in Neuenburg on Matthew 6: 9-13; Johann Penner [preached] in Chortitza; H. Penner in Osterwick. I lift up mine eyes to the hills from where comes my help.

A brotherhood meeting. Peter Reimer from Nieder Chortitza was excommunicated because of his many lies and his unbecoming lifestyle among the Russians. O Lord give him insight.

March 4

The potter Knelsen of Rosenthal was ordered to appear before the ministerial council. He had criticized his children's guardians, and had hired out [his children] in the Molotschna without their [the guardians'] permission. [Knelsen] left for the Molotschna when he received the summons. David Doerksen of Schoeneberg also presented a problem. Last year he chopped birchwood in the forest without permission. The Garden Commission fined him five rubles which he refused to pay. He was elected as a member of the village council for 1837, but refused to accept the position because he felt he had been treated unfairly. He promised to pay his fine and to accept his position and so the matter was amicably settled.

I presided at a wedding in Neuenberg at ? Jacob Reimer married Susanna Wiens. I hope this will be a good marriage.

March 7

I preached in Schoenhorst on Isaiah 53:4. Brother Johann Penner [preached] in Chortitza. O Lord, let your suffering and pain be always in my thoughts.

March 11

Thursday. The contending parties Pankratz and Thiessen from Nieder-Chortitza did not appear [before the ministerial council] and so there was no agenda.

March 13

I preached the funeral sermon for the little daughter Helena Thiessen at the Jacob Thiessen [residence] in Einlage. She died on March 10 at five in the morning. I said that she had gone to Jesus the friend of children. When I returned home in the evening we had a visitor, sister Hermann Friesen from ?

March 14

Peter Dyck preached in Chortitza on 1 Corinthians 1:30. Johann Penner preached in Osterwick. If you can't free yourself from the burden of sin, cast a glance upon Jesus. His suffering must permeate my soul.

A brotherhood meeting. J. Knelsen tried to excuse himself before the church. He claimed he was not experienced in these matters. He was requested to reconcile himself with the guardians and give heed to the [prevailing] regulations. What can one do with people like K. who don't want to learn or understand anything.

March 16

Good Friday. I preached a funeral sermon on 1 Corinthians ? in Schoenhorst, in the home of the departed sister Brandt. She died after a six-day illness on March 13, 6 PM. She reached the age of forty-seven years, eight months and nine days. She was married for twenty-seven years, seven months and five days. She gave birth to ten children of whom four died and six are living. She had three grandchildren. "For the wages of sin is death, but the gift of God is eternal life in Christ Jesus our Lord." (Rom. 6:23)

In the afternoon Bernd Rempel, our son David, H. Loepp as well as my brother-in-law Bernd Thiessen left for the Molotschna amidst rain. The angel of the Lord accompany them.

March 18

The first day of Easter. I preached in Neu-Osterwick on Mark 16: 1-8; elder J. Dyck [preached] in Chortitza; H. Penner in Burwalde; Peter Dyck in Schoenhorst; Johann Penner in Blumengart; J. Regier in Rosengart. The gift of God is eternal life.

Mr. H. Hiebert from Muensterberg together with his wife and his parents-in-law, the Peter Loewens from Ladekopp, arrived here for lunch. They spent the night at J. Dyck's.

March 19

The second day of Easter. I preached in Chortitza on Luke 24:13-36. Elder J. Dyck [preached] in Schoenhorst; Jacob Regier in Osterwick; brother Peter Dyck in Adelsheim. The Lord is truly risen and has appeared to us.

March 21

I preached the funeral sermon on Psalm 90:12 in the home of the departed Abraham Klassen of Chortitza. He died on March 18 at 4 PM following a ten-day illness. He reached the age of sixty-seven less a day. He married twice. His first marriage lasted thirty-one years, eight months and fourteen days. It produced twelve children, of whom eight died and four are living. He became a grandfather to twenty-six children, of whom nine died and seventeen are living. His second marriage lasted nine years, ten months and sixteen days. There were no children. Lord "teach us to number our days aright, that we may gain a heart of wisdom" (Psa. 90:12).

Toward evening my sister-in-law Mrs. H. Thiessen from ? came to visit with her children. They spent the night at the Peters.

March 22

The H. Hieberts and Peter Loewens of Ladekopp left after they visited their friends. The angel of the Lord accompany them. Our son-in-law also returned safe and sound. My cousin David Penner with his wife and daughter together with Claas Dyck from Rosenort arrived. They spent the night at our neighbour Cornelius Epp's.

March 23

In the morning we left to visit their children at our communal sheep farm.

March 25

I and elder Jacob Dyck presented the articles of faith to the congregation in Chortitza on March 2. Faith is a question of the heart. Create in me, O God, a clean heart.

March 28

We had several guests in the afternoon. S.K. and his wife from Einlage; Gerhard Dyck and his wife from Rudnerweide; the school teachers J. Fast from Pastwa and H. Franz from Gnadenfeld; Mrs. Abraham Rempel and Mrs ? from Gnadenfeld. These [ladies] spent the night in Einlage. In the evening cousin David Penner and his wife came from the communal sheep farm after attending the engagement of their daughter Gertrude to ? They spent the night at our house.

March 29

The David Penners began their return journey. The Lord accompany them. The teacher Johann W. from Rudnerweide was with us for lunch.

On Thursday Johann Harder from Rosenthal was asked to appear before the ministerial council. He had taken home a sheep and a lamb belonging to the communal flock. The sheep master Schmit was soon on his trail and seized the sheep and the lamb. Schmit asserted that a young sheep herder had called after Harder but he drove away. Harder said the animals had been far from the flock and that he intended to report the incident later. The council did not really believe Harder and so the matter was postponed until the Sunday brotherhood meeting.

Elder Jacob Warkentin from Altonau arrived last night with two other ministers to stay with elder J. Dyck. He too was present in the council room.

March 30

Elder David Warkentin, elder J. Dyck and both ministers came to visit brother H. Penner to view the *Privilegium.*[6] I was there too and conversed with them. The Lord go with them as they journey home.

May 1

I preached the funeral sermon on 1 Corinthians 15:30 for the baby H. Unger in Einlage in the home of the widow, Mrs. Abram Unger. He died on April 28 at 6 PM at the age of thirty weeks and two days. Such a child is of the kingdom of God.

May 2

Elder J. Dyck read the articles of faith (part II) for the third time. Eighty-four baptismal candidates both male and female were listed. Our son Diedrich was among them. O Lord Jesus, place his name in the book of life.

Johann Harder confessed his fault before the brotherhood, asked forgiveness and promised to better himself. He was forgiven. Lord, keep him on the right path throughout his life.

During the afternoon I preached a funeral sermon on Psalm 90:12 for our sister-in-law Catherina Thiessen in Schoenhorst at their home of Johann Loewen. She died on May 28 at 7 PM after a six-day illness. She was fifty-nine years of age. Her first marriage lasted almost two years. She had one child, who died. Her second marriage lasted twenty-eight years. She was the mother of six children, of whom two died and four are still alive. She had three grandchildren, one died and two are living. The Lord is gracious. He cares for all his creation.

May 3

On this Monday I and my dear wife with Helen, Ann and Abraham travelled to our sheep farm and returned safe and sound on May 5 in the evening. Thanks to the dear Saviour for his gracious care and protection.

May 6

My sister's son Bernhard Rempel as well as ? said goodbye in order to begin their journey to Prussia. The Lord send his angel to protect their going and coming. The dear people leave on May 10.

May 9

Elder Jacob Rempel presented the articles of faith to the congregation for the fourth time. There were thirteen additional candidates but one of them, H. Wiens from Einlage, the son of the deceased Abraham

Wiens, was rejected because of his dissipated lifestyle. In all there are ninety-six candidates. Grant true faith to these young hearts, O Lord.

During the afternoon my daughter, Mrs. Friesen, safely delivered a young son Henry. May the Lord allow him to develop for his honour and glory.

May 10

I travelled to Yekaterinoslav on business with Jacob, Henry and Johann. We returned safely on May 12. Thank you Lord Jesus for your protection and leading.

My brother-in-law H. Thiessen is drinking heavily.... God knows when he will stop.

May 14

My brother-in-law, J. Peters from Fuerstenau, was our guest for a few hours.

The funeral sermon for Mrs. Guenther in Neuendorf was held in their home. She died on May 12 after a lengthy illness and was very sick for the last three days. She reached the age of forty-four years, nine weeks and one day. She was married for twenty-five years and gave birth to seven sons and four daughters, of whom four sons and one daughter died. Those who die in the Lord will not see death.

May 16

Elder J. Dyck presented the articles of faith for the fifth time. The youth J. Wiens of Einlage was also accepted as a candidate by the congregation. Blessed are those who accept a name which "no one but he himself knows" (Rev. 19:12).

The ministerial council met on Thursday to consider the case of the Einlage resident Schutzmann and three young men whom he had brought before the district council for perpetrating mischief against him. The district council had sentenced them to manual (?) labour. Schutzmann was reminded that members of the church first bring such issues to the ministerial council and if they cannot be resolved they are turned over to the district office.

During the night our daughter Mrs. Peter Rempel in Schoenhorst gave birth to a son called Heinrich. May the parents raise the child to the glory of God.

May 17

Travelled to the sheep farm with our children Jacob, Heinrich and Johann in order to shear the sheep.

May 20

J. Rempel appeared before the ministerial council. He became intoxicated and got into a squabble with N. Harder who twice slapped him across the ears. They were questioned, reconciled themselves to one another and asked forgiveness and were dismissed. "Blessed is the man who does not walk in the counsel of the wicked or stand in the way of scorners." (Psa. 1:1)

J. Regier of Altonau and his wife Margareta, the daughter of David Penner from Ohrloff, arrived as guests on our sheep farm.

May 22

I and our children returned from the sheep farm safe and sound. Thank you, O Lord, for all your blessing.

May 23

Elder J. Dyck catechised some sixty-five baptismal candidates in the Chortitza church. In accordance with the instructions of the ministerial council and decision of the congregation I catechised thirty baptismal candidates in the Neuendorf church. It was the first time that a service was held in the church and so I preached a short inauguration sermon on ?. The Lord blessed the proceedings to his glory and the salvation of our souls. There were twelve youths and eighteen young ladies.

May 26

Johann Regier left. The Lord be with him.

May 27

Ascension Day. I preached in Neuendorf on Mark 16:19 and catechised the baptismal candidates, twelve youths and eighteen young ladies. The catechising and the sermon lasted three hours. In Chortitza elder J. Dyck preached on the theme "Our walk is in Heaven." He catechised sixty-five baptismal candidates. Praise and thanks to the Lord Jesus.

May 28

On Friday, I, my brother-in-law Abraham Friesen and our son Jacob left for the annual fair in Charkov in the company of H. Isaak from Rosenthal and his son Abraham. We arrived there on June 3. There was a great deal of wool on the market and the prices were low and unsettled.

June 7

Pentecost. We attended a Lutheran church [in Charkov]. The sermon was weak in content and delivered so rapidly that we were able to understand little of it. A child was baptized after the sermon.

June 8

I sold my wool at thirty-five kopecks a *pud* for washed wool. It came to five rubles and twenty-three kopecks in silver currency.[7] Abraham Isaak and Abraham Friesen could not sell the community wool and had to place it in a warehouse. Apparently some 45,000 *pud* were stored in this fashion. The highest prices for the washed wool was forty-two kopecks per *pud*, the lowest twenty-eight kopecks per *pud*.

June 9

This evening we began our return journey and arrived home safe and sound on June 13. Thank the Lord for his guidance and protection.

Events During My Absence

May 30

Elder J. Dyck presented the articles of faith to the congregation for the sixth time. The baptismal candidates sat on the front benches. The young ladies, as was customary, had braided their hair.

June 6

During the first day of Pentecost elder J. Dyck preached in Chortitza, Johann Penner in Neuendorf.

June 7

Elder J. Dyck administered holy baptism to sixty-five candidates in Chortitza. Our son Diedrich was among them. O Holy Jesus, baptize him with your Holy Spirit, like all who have received baptism.

June 13

Elder J. Dyck administered holy baptism to fifty candidates in Neuendorf. Baptize them in Your death unto eternal life.

Brother H. Penner preached the preparatory sermon in Chortitza. Prepare us all as worthy guests for your table.

June 20

Elder J. Dyck administered Holy Communion in the Chortitza church for 341 congregational members. Jesus, You Son of David, have mercy on me. Brother H. Penner preached the preparatory sermon in Neuendorf. Be with us all, Lord Jesus, for the sake of your eternal love. Amen.

June 22

I held the funeral sermon for Anna, the infant daughter of Johann Penner of Einlage. She died at 5 AM after a four-week illness at the age of one year and four days. Blessed are such little ones for they die in the Lord. I spoke on Hebrews 13.

June 28

Elder J. Dyck celebrated Holy Communion with 294 congregational members in Neuendorf. J. Loewen preached the thanksgiving sermon [communion] on 1 Peter 2:24. Praise and thanks to you, O Holy Jesus, for all the blessings you bestow upon us.

July 2

Dr. H.V. Grosheim arrived here to become our doctor.

July 4

Brother J. Regier preached in Chortitza. I preached the thanksgiving sermon on Ephesians 1:3 in Neuendorf. H. Penner preached the thanksgiving sermon in Osterwick. In Neuendorf I announced that services would be held only every second Sunday. Thank the Lord for He is good and his love endures for ever. Amen.

At 5 PM Dr Grosheim left for his return journey. In the evening Johann Klassen arrived from Yekaterinoslav.

July 5

Johann Klassen left for his return journey. The Lord's angel accompany him!

July 7

His excellency Count Tolstoi arrived in Neuhorst and spent the night there.

July 8

[He] spent two hours in Neuendorf and some time in Chortitza, then left for Mariupol.

July 11

His excellency returned to Einlage and Neuendorf where he was received by elder J. Dyck and ? Janzen. Elder J. Dyck thanked him for all the benevolence of the government and commended us to the government. He requested more settlement land near Mariupol and a loan from the Fund for Settlers. The discussion lasted about seven minutes. His excellency had been sent as a representative of the Minister of the Interior.

On Sunday Jacob Regier preached in Chortitza on 1 John 5:6. The blood of Jesus Christ, God's Son, cleanses us from all sin. Amen.

July 14

I preached a funeral sermon on Hebrews 13:14 for the deceased brother Claas Kroeker in the family home in Chortitza. He was sick for twelve and one-half days. He lived for fifty-three years, three months and twenty-six days. He fathered five sons and three daughters, of whom three sons and two daughters are still alive.

July 15

On Thursday Dirk Braun from Einlage appeared before the ministerial council. He had not weeded his portion in the village plantation and the yard of the district office on time. He acknowledged his transgression and promised to improve in the future. He asked the chairperson Siemens to forgive him and promised to make peace with the village council.

Johann Friesen, who is living on rented land outside of the colony, informed elder Jacob Dyck through his brother Isaak Friesen that he intended to shoot Peter Driedger from N. when the first opportunity presented itself. Driedger had often insulted him. He was keeping a loaded weapon hidden in the manure pile. Both parties were brought [before the ministerial council]. Isaak Friesen affirmed the above story as true, though some details varied. He made the following statement [on behalf of his brother]

1. Driedger asserted that Friesen's wife preferred him.

2. Driedger had received permission from elder Jacob Dyck to [charge interest]? for the 600 rubles he had given Friesen.

3. Driedger asserted that the deceased parents of Friesen had been thieves. Driedger could not recall doing so but admitted that he had often insulted Friesen with his talk. He promised to refrain from making unwelcome remarks and seek to change his relationship with Friesen. Driedger finally admitted his sin and reconciled himself with Friesen. How the light of the Gospel has been obscured in so many folk? When will the beautiful dawn of true enlightenment begin to break among us? The Lord only knows.

July 18

Elder J. Dyck preached in Chortitza on Matthew 7:13, 14. Brother Peter Dyck [preached] in Neuendorf. Help me, O Lord Jesus, to enter through the narrow gate.

A brotherhood meeting [was held] in Chortitza. The congregation decided to levy two rubles per farmstead in order to complete both churches [Chortitza and Neuendorf]. Furthermore each male congregational member would be levied one ruble, each female member fifty kopecks. Any non-resident member or associate member who does not wish to contribute should withdraw from the congregation.

Does the congregation wish to employ Dr. V. Grosheim for 2,000 rubles per year? Most were in favour but the matter was unresolved.

The congregation was encouraged to obey the regulations of the church. Watchman, when will the night end?

July 25

I preached in Einlage on Matthew 20: 2-3. Elder J. Dyck preached in Chortitza; J. Regier [preached] in Osterwick. The Lord is near to all those who call upon him.

July 28

I preached the funeral sermon for little Maria Neustaedter in the home of Johann Neustaedter of Einlage. She died on May 26, 8.30 AM after a five-day illness at the age of twenty days. Blessed are the dead who die in the Lord. Their angels continuously see the face of their Father in heaven.

July 31

I preached in Chortitza on Acts 24:25. Elder J. Dyck [preached] in Neuendorf. Without repentance and holiness no one can see the Lord.

Goerz from Rosenthal was invited into the ministerial room. He had fought with one of the colonists and quarrelled with several others. He apologized and was dismissed.

Johann Siemens of Nieder-Chortitza had again broken the regulations governing the village plantation. He asked the chairperson of the village council for forgiveness and promised obedience in the future. He was then dismissed. O Lord Jesus, have mercy on us all.

August 8

I preached in Chortitza on Luke 15: 12-24. Elder J. Dyck [preached] in Neu-Osterwick. Peter Dyck preached in Schoenhorst. The Son of Man is come to seek and to save what was lost.

August 14

I travelled to our sheep farm and since the administrator D.P. could not agree with Rempel—it concerned 200 *dessiatines*[8] of [rented]? land —I made the following proposal:

I was prepared to leave the rented land in April, 1938, provided the nobleman agrees to accept Rempel as a renter or he could vacate [his 200 *dessiatines*] or we could divide the land in question [400 *dessiatines* in total]. Rempel decided to vacate on the fifteenth [August?].

August 15

H. Penner preached in Chortitza, Johann Penner in Neuendorf. Blessed is the man who does not walk in the ways of the ungodly.

August 17
Arrived home safe and sound from the sheep farm. Thank you, Saviour, for your love and faithfulness.

August 18
Ens and his wife from Tiegenhagen and cousin Cornelius Epp from Schoenfeld were at our house for coffee. Ens left for Schoenwiese while cousin Epp stayed with my brother-in-law. He left on August 19. The Lord's angel protect you dear ones.

August 19
On Thursday Abraham Dyck of Neuendorf appeared before the ministerial council.

August 22
H. Penner preached in Chortitza on 1 John 4;10. Brother Johann Penner [preached] in Neu-Osterwick. Lord Jesus, give me and everyone strength in the struggle against sin.

August 29
Johann Penner preached in Chortitza, H. Penner [preached] in Neuendorf. He who has begun the good work in you will bring it to completion.

September 5
Brother Johann Penner preached in Chortitza on John 5:28, 29. H. Penner [preached] in Neu-Osterwick. He gives his sheep eternal life. O Lord, I am your sheep. Find me a faithful shepherd.

September 9
Thursday. Several members of the village council were brought before the ministerial council—Herman Wall, Peter Regier and the farmer Daniel Loewen. Loewen was accused of disobedience, swearing and cursing, and of drinking too much whisky, which accounted for his behaviour. He promised to stop drinking forthwith. Both parties were reconciled and parted in peace. Elder J. Dyck had travelled to Molotschna. I, brother P. Dyck and a deacon were present. O God,

protect Loewen from madness. Forgive him his sins and lead him in pathways where he will not falter.

September 12

I preached in Neuendorf on 1 John 4. Peter Dyck preached in Chortitza. Bless these meditations to our souls' salvation, Lord Jesus.

In the evening cousin D.P. and his daughter Elisabeth came from ?. They spent the night at my neighbour C. Epp's.

September 13

In the morning cousin D.P. travelled to the community sheep farm. Brother J. Penner from Muensterberg dropped in for a half-hour visit during the afternoon.

September 14

Cousin D.P. and his daughter and son-in-law left for their return journey. May the angels watch over them.

In the evening P. Loewen, his wife and children as well as Anna came for a visit. They stayed with Jacob Dyck. Commit your way to the Lord, trust in Him and He will bring it to pass (Psa. 37:5).

September 22

During the morning the P. Loewens left for Yekaterinoslav. In the afternoon I preached a funeral sermon on 1 Corinthians 15:30 for a small deceased daughter in the home of Isaak. She died on September 14 at 7:30 AM after an illness of three weeks, at the age of one year, four months and twenty days. Jesus accepts the children.

September 25

We and Mr. Peter Loewen visited our children in Schoenhorst.

September 26

Brother Jacob Braun preached in Chortitza on Matthew 5:6. Peter Dyck [preached] in Neuendorf.

This afternoon the Peter Loewens began their return journey. The Lord's angel guide you dear ones.

September 30

? safely returned to Einlage from his journey to Prussia. He brought with him his brother-in-law Johann Rempel and his family from Koenigsberg as well as the school teacher Wilhelm Lange from ?.

October 1

Crown prince Alexander Nikolayevich, the heir to the throne, passed by on the road from Nikopol to Yekaterinoslav via Kanzerovka.

October 3

I preached a harvest and thanksgiving sermon on Acts 14:17 in Neuendorf. Elder J. Dyck [preached] in Chortitza and Jacob Regier in Neu-Osterwick. Those who sow in tears will reap with joy.

In the morning the David Rempels and their son Bernhard left for the return trip to Prussia.

October 6

This morning at 6 AM I, together with our son David, and daughter Lenchen, left for Yekaterinoslav to see the tsarina and her daughter, the grand duchess Maria. We arrived at my brother-in-law's at 2 PM. The second wagon carried elder J. Dyck, Jacob Hildebrand together with Siemens and his wife from Chortitza. The third wagon carried J. von Kampen, Peter Siemens Senior and two secretarial assistants from the district office, David Hamm and Wilhelm Penner....[9]

October 8

This evening we arrived home safe and sound. Thank you, Lord Jesus.

October 10

Jacob Regier preached in Chortitza, Jacob Braun in Neuendorf. The Lord bless these sermons to his honour and glory.

October 15

This Friday at 2 PM his illustrious majesty passed through Neuenburg and Einlage with nine wagons.[10]

October 17

Brother Jacob Regier preached in Chortitza. Brother H. Penner [preached] in Neuendorf, brother Jacob Braun in Neu-Osterwick. We plant in hope.

October 20

His excellency V. J.?, who was accompanying his exalted majesty through the Molotschna colonies, stopped here and made elder Jacob Dyck's home his chief residence.

October 21

His excellency continued his journey to Odessa. The Lord's angel accompany him.

October 24

Elder J. Dyck preached in Chortitza on Matthew 7:13, 14. Regier [preached] in Neuendorf. Be the guide on my path of life, O Lord Jesus. Amen.

October 31

Elder Jacob Dyck preached in Chortitza. ? [preached] in Neuendorf, J. Braun in Osterwick. The Lord's Word does not return empty-handed.

Elder Jacob Dyck, brother W. Penner and J. Braun left for the Bergthal settlement this afternoon. They want to celebrate communion and engage in some discussions. The Lord's angel accompany you.

November 7

I preached in Chortitza on Ephesians 3:18. Peter Dyck [preached] in Neuendorf. O Lord Jesus let us see what is important to our soul's salvation, let us grasp you in true faith.

November 8

This evening elder J. Dyck and his travel companions returned from the new Bergthal settlement, where they celebrated communion.

November 13

My sister Anna has come to live with us for as long as it pleases her.

November 14

I preached on Acts 10:45 in Chortitza. Brother H. Penner [preached] in Neuendorf, elder J. Dyck in Osterwick. Without faith it is impossible to please God.

November 15
During the evening ? Thiessens from Yekaterinoslav arrived for a visit.

November 18
The Thiessens left this morning and took three hired men with them.

Afternoon I officiated at the wedding of Johann Schmit and Elisabet Esau at the home of my neighbour Martin Schmit. May the Lord's blessing rest upon this couple.

November 21
I preached in Neuendorf on Luke 18:10. H. Penner preached in Chortitza.

Brotherhood meeting. Peter Penner and his wife from Rosengart were excommunicated because they slept together before they were married, while he was a widower and she not yet baptized. Similarly, the bachelor J. Dyck had an affair with the blacksmith's wife and his wife in turn committed adultery with A.K. in Burwalde. Lord, be merciful to us as sinners!

On November 18 the brothers Jacob and Franz Thiessen and David Isaac appeared before the ministerial council on account of gossip. They finally reconciled. In Neu-Osterwick there was a quarrel regarding the sale of a horse. The matter remained unresolved. Everyone wants to give orders but no one wants to listen or be taught.

November 23
I met Dr. H.V. Grosheim who will be opening an independent practice in Neuenburg. He moved into the rented quarters near Isaak Braun. Will we know how to value a doctor?

November 24
I and our son Jacob travelled to Yekaterinoslav where we arrived at the Thiessens at 5 PM. The steppe was covered with snow, but we drove by wagon.

November 27
I preached in Osterwick on the first advent. My text was Isaiah 9:9. J. Braun preached in Neuendorf. Prepare our hearts.

A brotherhood meeting. Abraham Klassen of Burwalde was accepted as a member of the church. J. Dyck and his wife were not accepted. Watchman, when will the night end?

December 2

I officiated at the marriage of H. Toews and Margareta Loewen at the home of David Loewen in Chortitza. The Lord's blessing rest upon this couple!

On November 28 Peter Penner and his wife from Rosengart were accepted as church members by elder J. Dyck. The Lord grant them repentance for their sins.

December 5

On the second advent I preached in Neuenburg on Revelation 1: 7, 8. Johann Penner [preached] in Chortitza; H. Penner in Neuendorf.

December 9

? appeared before the ministerial council for illicit sexual activity.

My brother-in-law Friesen dropped by for lunch. Afternoon I officiated at the wedding of Johann Wiens and Susanna Dyck at the home of Jacob Dyck, who is a miller in Osterwick. The Lord's blessing accompany this couple.

December 10

This afternoon the H. Friesens commenced their return journey. The Lord be with them.

I held the funeral sermon on Acts 22:7 for little Anna Loewen, the daughter of my neighbour D. Loewen. She died on December 6 at 11 PM following an illness of eleven days. She was one year, two weeks old. Let the little children come unto me and prevent them not.

December 12

Johann Penner preached in Chortitza on John 1: 6-14. H. Penner [preached] in Neu-Osterwick, Jacob Regier in Neuendorf.

Brotherhood meeting. Jacob Waerner and ? were excommunicated from the congregation for adultery. "He will clear his threshing floor — burning up the chaff with unquenchable fire." (Matt. 3:12)

December 19

Peter Dyck preached in Chortitza. Johann Penner preached in Neuendorf. May the Lord bless these proclamations.

Brotherhood meeting. Mrs. ? was accepted as a member of the congregation by elder J. Dyck. Jesus accepts sinners. ? were excommunicated from the congregation for adultery. The end result of such a lifestyle is death.

December 25

On the first day of Christmas I preached in Schoenhorst on John 1:14. Elder J. Dyck [preached] in Chortitza; H. Penner in Neuendorf; Peter Dyck in Osterwick; J. P[enner] in Burwalde; J. Regier in ?. Jesus is my Saviour.

December 26

On the second day of Christmas I preached in Osterwick on ?. Elder J. Dyck preached in Neuendorf. The Lord is near to all who earnestly call upon his name.

Thank God the year has ended. "Because of the Lord's great love we are not consumed, for his compassions never fail." (Lamentations 3:22) "Praise the Lord O my soul; all my inmost being praise his holy name—He forgives all my sins and heals all my diseases." (Psa. 103: 1, 3)

During the past year the Chortitza and Schoenwieser congregations saw the birth of one hundred and forty-five males, one hundred and thirty-two females, totalling two hundred and seventy-seven children. There were eighty-two deaths, thirty-nine males, forty-three females. Some one hundred and ninety-five children survived. There were forty-eight marriages.

The past winter was reasonably mild with relatively little snow. With the coming of spring the snow melted in a few days and the runoff caused considerable damage. Spring and early summer were productive, late summer and fall very dry. The rye did not establish itself too well. Winter began after St. Martin's day (November 11). There was little snow and the temperatures dropped to minus 22°. The hay and grain harvest was rather good. Hay could not be sold. Rye sold at five to six rubles [per *pud*]; wheat at ten rubles; barley at two and one-half to three rubles; oats at two to two and one-half rubles; millet four to four and one-half rubles; peas six to eight rubles; potatoes three to ? rubles; butter twenty to twenty-two kopecks per pound; washed wool [sold for] eighteen to thirty rubles per *pud*; slaughter sheep seven to nine and one-half rubles; breeding sheep ten to twelve rubles each; female lambs five to six rubles each; male lambs four to five rubles.

The life of the church was rather tranquil. There were no cases of theft or even rumours of it. In Rosengart, sexual sins and adultery, long hidden, have suddenly come to the fore. Such issues were unheard of until now. Watch and pray that you fall not into temptation.

There was a split in the life of the church. Elder Peter Wedel was abandoned by his congregation. Oh God take charge and have mercy upon these erring ones.

Endnotes

This section of the diary was first published as "1837: A Year in the Life of David Epp," in the Journal of the American Historical Society of Germans from Russia, *Vol. 20, No.2 (Summer, 1997), pp. 1-12. I want to thank the* Journal *for permission to reprint it.*

[1] Temperatures were measured according to the Réaumur scale between 1830 and 1918. The French naturalist established the freezing point at 0°R and the boiling point at 80°R. A Réaumur degree equals 1.25 Celsius.

[2] The practice of preaching a preparatory sermon (*Vorbereitungspredigt*) on the Sunday prior to communion originated in Prussia. Custom dictated that the elder administrate the ordinance. On the Sunday following communion a sermon of praise and thanks (*Dankpredigt*) was preached.

[3] The *Volost* or *Gebietsamt* was an administrative district comprising several villages. It was the equivalent of a county, municipality or district in North American terms.

[4] The *Anwohner* usually owned no farm land in the village and either rented or owned his dwelling. Such a person could have been a craftsman or agricultural labourer. By the 1870s this landless population generated an economic crisis in the Russian Mennonite colonies which was eventually solved by emigration to North America and colonization within Russia.

[5] The full title of this Guardian Committee was "Das Fuersorge Komitee der auslaendischer Kolonisten Sued-Russlands."

[6] The term *Privilegium* referred to the terms of settlement under which the Mennonites entered Russia. The document was issued by Tsar Paul I in 1800. In addition they were governed by several decrees issued in 1763 by Empress Catherine II in the hopes of attracting foreign settlers.

[7] A *pud* is equivalent to 16.38 kilograms or 36.11 lbs. There are 100 kopecks to the ruble.

[8] A *dessiatine* equals 1.0925 hectares or 2.7 acres.

[9] Epp notes he left a special description of the royal visit to Yekaterinoslav, but it is not part of the surviving manuscript.

[10] It is not clear whether this refers to the crown prince.

1838

January 1

"Whatever you ask for in prayer, believe you will receive and it will come to pass" [Matt. 21:22]. I preached in Neuendorf on Ephesians 4:22-24. Elder Jacob Dyck preached in Chortitza, H. Penner in Schoenhorst, Jacob Braun in Neuosterwick, ? , Johann Penner in Einlage. Renew our hearts and minds, O Lord Jesus, to Your glory.

January 2

Jacob Braun preached in Chortitza and Peter Dyck in Neuendorf. "When your judgements come upon the earth, the people of the world learn righteousness" [Isa. 26:9].

Bruederschaft. The wife of Johann Penner of Neuendorf; Jacob Dyck and his wife; the wife of Martin Penner; Wilhelm Thiessen from Rosengart and Claas Krahn of Kronsthal—all were excommunicated from the congregation on account of adultry and fornication. Today they were readmitted as members in the congregation by elder Jacob Dyck. "Or do you show contempt for the riches of his kindness, tolerance and patience, not realizing that God's kindness leads you toward repentance?" [Rom. 2:4].[1]

January 6

Elder Jacob Dyck preached in Chortitza. P. Dyck preached in Neuendorf, J. Braun in Osterwick. "Arise, shine, for your light has come, and the glory of the Lord arises upon you." [Isa. 60:1]

January 9

I preached in Neuendorf on Acts 24:25. J. Braun preached in Chortitza, Peter Dyck in Osterwick. "Today, if you hear his voice, do not harden you hearts...." [Psa. 95:8] The unrepentent sinner will receive a harsh and severe judgement.

January 11

Tuesday at 10:30 PM with the temperature at minus 11° we experienced an earthquake which ran west to east and lasted *one* minute. The windows clattered, the shutters clapped and the furniture and dishes moved and rattled. The cattle in their stalls were restless and the feathered flocks fell to the ground. The earthquake came with a sound like the rush of a mighty wind. Who does not recognize the power and goodness of God in this event? Praise and thanks my Saviour for your protection.

January 16

J. Regier preached in Chortitza. J. Braun preached in Neuendorf, H. Penner in Neuenberg.

Bruederschaft. Regarding Mrs. Jacob Wiebe from Rosengart who committed adultery with Abraham Penner.... They had been excommunicated on January 9 and were readmitted into the congregation by elder Jacob Dyck. Lord do not lead us sinners into judgement.

January 20

Jacob B. and ? appeared before the *Lehrdienst* on Thursday. They had shot a fox together and sold the fur. Then they had a sharp disagreement and came to blows. They reconciled and departed in peace. Only those who are truly the children of God and are led by God's Spirit truly avoid evil.

January 23

Brother J. Regier preached in Chortitza on 1 Peter 5:11. H. Penner preached in Neuendorf, J. Braun in Neu-Osterwick. God does not wish that any should perish but that all convert and have eternal life.

January 27

Peter Driediger from Neuendorf, D. Thiessen and Johann Braun from Schoenhorst and Gerhard Braun from Neu-Osterwick appeared before the *Lehrdienst* on Thursday. They got drunk at the August fair in Nikopol and danced, cavorted and engaged in misconduct. They had drawn in Claas Dyck of Osterwick, but he was not at fault. The matter will be dealt with by the *Bruederschaft* following holy communion.

The young man Heinrich Koslowsky had an affair with a young lady. This too was referred to the *Bruederschaft*. When love grows cold, godlessness takes over.

January 30

Elder Jacob Dyck preached the preparatory sermon [for communion] in Chortitza on Psalm ? P. Dyck preached in Neuendorf, J. Regier in Osterwick. Prepare us all O Lord to be worthy guests at your table.

February 3

I presided at the marriage of Peter Epp and Sara Wieler at the Chortitza residence of Johann Wieler. Lord give them strength to walk in your ways.

February 6

Elder Jacob Dyck celebrated holy communion with two hundred and eighty members of the congregation. His text was I Corinthians 11:23-29. H. Penner preached the preparatory sermon in Neuendorf. You give power to the weak and strength to the feeble.

February 13

I preached the thanksgiving sermon for holy communion in Chortitza on Ephesians 1:3. Elder Jacob Dyck celebrated holy communion with two hundred and fifty-one members in Neuendorf. "Because of the Lord's great love we are not consumed, for his compassions never fail" [Lam 3:22].

February 20

I preached in Chortitza on Acts 4:11-12. H. Penner preached the thanksgiving sermon in Neuendorf. J. Braun preached in Neu-Osterwick. Whoever believes in Jesus will not be put to shame.

Note for February 17

I presided at the marriage of Jacob Braun from Schoeneberg and Catarina Werner at the Chortitza residence of Peter Werner. The Lord's peace go with them.

February 27

I preached in Neuendorf on Isaiah 53:4. H. Penner preached in Chortitza. Christ came from God for our wisdom, righteousness and salvation. O God, be gracious to us for Jesus' sake.

Bruederschaft in Chortitza. The following were excommunicated from the congregation: Peter Driedger from Neuendorf; Olfert Doerksen, Thiessen, J. Braun, D. Redekopp, Bernhard Giesbrecht from the community sheep farm; G. Braun and P. Siemens from Neu-Osterwick; H. Koslowsky from Einlage. When will this dissolute, wild life in the community end? Convert us, O Lord, so that we are truly converted.

March 3

The following appeared before the *Lehrdienst* on Thursday on charges of excessive liquor drinking and violence: Peter Harder; Peter Thiessen; Wilhelm Doerksen and the pub keeper Olfert from Schoenhorst; H. Dyck and Winter Stellmacher from Einlage; J. Friesen from a private farm [*chutor*]. The matter was referred to the *Bruederschaft* on Sunday. The lightning flashes, the thunder rolls. God be merciful to us sinners![2]

March 4

I met my brother-in-law H. Thiessen and his wife from Yekaterinoslav at Johann Siemens'. The reason: our dear grandfather had become very ill. I had left for the community farm on Febrary 28 and returned this evening.

March 6

I preached in Neu-Osterwick on Isaiah 53:7. H. Penner preached in Chortitza, J. Penner in Neuendorf. Lord let your pain and suffering be constantly on my mind.

Bruederschaft in Chortitza. Bernard Giesbrecht and D. Redekopp (see February 27) were readmitted as members of the congregation by elder Jacob Dyck. Have mercy on them, O Jesus.

The following were excommunicated for various offences: D. Rempel; Peters; Thiessen; Friesen for ?; Mrs. Johann Penner for adultery; J. Friesen from the private farm [*chutor*] for drunkenness and violence; Winter from Einlage; Martin Penner from Rosengart was excommunicated for sodomy; Peter Harder from Schoenhorst for ? Those who sow in the flesh will reap eternal damnation in the flesh if they do not repent. Give us, O Lord Jesus, the strength to direct our energies to the voice of the Spirit so that we through your grace may partake of eternal blessing.

March 9

My brother-in-law left at 5 AM for his return journey. May an angel accompany him and his family.

March 10

Dirk Braun of Einlage appeared before the *Lehrdienst* because he gave a tongue lashing to Jacob Thiessen. He [Thiessen] refused to tolerate Braun's behaviour and had complained to elder Jacob Dyck.

There was also the case of Peter Rempel and his stepdaughter Maria, who is now engaged to be married. The Rempels and their daughter had gotten an older bachelor, Cornelius Jans, drunk with liquor with the intent of getting him to marry Maria. According to Jans she had come to him in the barn and carried on with him until midnight. Later Jans, tormented by his conscience, tried to commit suicide but was prevented from doing so by Maria. Later she asked him if he had told anyone about it and he said no. She had begged him to keep quiet and he promised to do so. If, however, she decided to get married he would tell all. Maria denied having an affair. The matter will be presented to the congregation [*Bruederschaft*] on Sunday. When will the night of sin vanish?

March 13

Brother J. Penner preached in Chortitza, H. Penner in Neuendorf. Make us your true disciples, O Lord.

The following were admitted to the congregation by elder Jacob Dyck: Mrs. J. Penner and Jacob Peters from Schoenhorst; Peter Driedger from Neuendorf; Gerhard Braun and Abraham Friesen from Osterwick; H. Koslowsky; Johann W. and H. Dyck from Einlage; Martin Penner from Rosengart. Those from the various private farms included Olfert, Johann Doerksen, Johann Braun, D. Thiessen and Penner, whom the orthodox clergy was not permitted to accept. O Lord, have mercy on us.

March 14

I preached the funeral sermon on ? for the child Margareta Peters at the residence of Aron Peters in Neu-Osterwick. She died on March 11, 8 PM at the age of eighteen days. Blessd are such little ones for they die in the Lord.

March 15

My brother-in-law Peter Loewen and my sister-in-law Mrs. D. Thiessen from Altonau came to visit our sick grandfather.

March 17

Olfert and his father-in-law Gerhard Enss from Schoenhorst appeared before the *Lehrdienst* on Thursday regarding a dispute about the farm. They reached an understanding and were reconciled.

Abraham Loepky from Nieder-Chortitza had made a lewd remark about Dyck now living in Blumengart. He is the son of H. Dyck from Nieder Chortitza. He admitted it and the matter was referred to the *Bruederschaft* on Sunday. Godlessness increases and love grows cold.

March 18

My brother-in-law P. Loewen and sister-in-law Thiessen began their return journey [to Altonau].

March 20

This morning our children moved to our community farm located on the land rented from H. Cromida. May the peace of Jesus be with them.

In Chortitza elder J. Dyck presented the articles of faith to the congregation for the first time. I did the same in Neuendorf. O Lord Jesus give us strength to keep the faith.

Bruederschaft. Dietrich Rempel and Peter Harder from Schoenhorst and D. Braun from Einlage were readmitted as members of the congregation. When will these men stop drinking? Lord, You know. Have mercy on them.

March 27

On this Palm Sunday I preached in Neuendorf on Matthew 21:1-9. Peter Dyck preached in Chortitza. Enter my heart and all our hearts, O Lord Jesus. Make my heart Your dwelling, Your temple. Amen.

Bruederschaft in Chortitza. Wilhelm Friesen of Schoenhorst was accepted as a member of the congregation by elder Jacob Dyck. O Lord, Jesus, free all the captives.

Note: On March 20 Loepky had to appear before the congregation on account of slander. He asked for forgiveness and was reconciled with his opponent. The matter was resolved. O Holy Jesus, open all our eyes.

April 2

The H. Thiessens and their children left on their return journey. The Lord's angel go with them. The first day of Easter. I preached in Chortitza on Mark 16:1-8. Peter Dyck preached in Neuendorf, elder Jacob Dyck in Schoenhorst. I search for you, Lord Jesus. Let your grace become my righteousness. The congregation prayed for my old father-in-law Thiessen, who is very ill. My Lord Jesus have mercy on him.

April 4

On this second day of Easter I preached in Neuendorf on Luke 24:13-36. Elder Jacob Dyck preached in Chortitza on Mark 16:1-8. J. Regier preached in Neuendorf. No one was available for Osterwick. Heal me! Jesus accepts sinners.

April 10

I presented the articles of faith for the second time in Neuendorf. Elder Jacob Dyck presented them to the congregation in Chortitza.

Bruederschaft in Neuendorf. It was decided to present the baptismal candidates from Neuendorf, Schoenhorst and ? in Neuendorf. A similar decision was made in Chortitza. J. Wall from Neuhorst was, on the basis of his own confession of sodomy during his youth, excommunicated from the congregation. Dear Lord Jesus make all things work together for good.

April 17

I presented the articles of faith to the Neuendorf congregation for the third time. The candidates were presented for the first time. There were twenty-seven persons of both genders.

Here in Chortitza elder Jacob Dyck presented the articles to the congregation for the third time. There were fifty baptismal candidates.

I presided over my first *Bruederschaft*. Bless, Lord Jesus, the beginning and the end. Johann Wall from Neuhorst was accepted as a member of the congregation by elder Jacob Dyck. Grace! Grace! Grace!

April 24

I presented the articles of faith to the congregation in Neuendorf for the fourth time. The baptismal candidates were presented for a second time—there were thirty-one persons of both genders. Elder Jacob Dyck presented the articles for the fourth time in Chortitza. Here there were fifty-eight baptismal candidates. Everything is dependent upon God's blessing.

May 1

I presented the articles of faith to the Neuendorf congregation for the fifth time. The thirty-one baptismal candidates were approved for holy baptism by the *Bruederschaft*. Write these names as all of ours, into Your book of eternal life.

May 3

On Tuesday my father-in-law Heinrich Thiessen died quietly at 12 noon following a nine-week illness. He reached the age of eighty-two years, seven months and two days. His illness was a difficult one. He suffered from a urinary disorder and a severe cough. He fought a difficult yet brave battle and his end was peaceable. He will receive joy for his sorrow and the oil of gladness for his troubled spirit. He so wished to die and be with Christ. Christ in His grace will fulfill his wish and prayer.

He was a widower for five years and three months. He was married for forty-eight years and twenty-eight days. He sired ten children, eight of whom died. He was a grandfather to thirty children, eight of whom died. Rest in peace, you noble spirit, until the end of time. A farewell to you, yet never will we be parted.

May 7

Our dear grandfather was buried in the Chortitza cemetary, where he will rest until the resurrection. H. Penner preached the funeral sermon. The Molotschna friends included: Dirksen, his wife and daughter from Tiege; my brother-in-law Abraham Warkentin and his wife; Mr. and Mrs. Claas Hildebrand and their son Peter from Muensterberg.

May 8

I catechized thirty-one baptismal candidates [in Neuendorf]. Elder Jacob Dyck catechized fifty-six [baptismal candidates] in Chortitza. Two persons in Bergthal were catechized by Jacob Braun. O Lord Jesus, grant that what these youngsters confess with their mouth they will also believe with their whole hearts.

May 9

The H. Thiessens and their children left on their return journey. The Lord's angel accompany them.

May 10

The Molotschna friends left at 1 PM. May the angel go with you.

I preached the funeral sermon for Jacob Dyck, our one-time neighbour in Chortitza, in the home of Abraham Wiebe. He died on May 7, 9 AM after a lengthy illness. He died in the seventy-sixth year of his life. He was married three times. His first marriage lasted one year and the child he sired soon died. His second marriage lasted twenty-four years. He sired eight children, five of whom died. His third marriage lasted twenty-three and a half years but produced no children. He was a grandfather to thirty-eight children, fourteen of whom died. Rest in peace, you noble man, until the end of time.

May 12

On Ascension Day I preached in Neuendorf on Mark 16:50-52. I catechized the baptismal candidates for a second time—there were thirteen young men and eighteen young women. In Chortitza elder J. Dyck preached on the theme "Our Walk is in Heaven." He catechized the baptismal candidates a second time. There were fifty-six persons. "How can a young man (and woman) keep their ways pure? By living according to your word." [Psa. 119:9].

May 15

I presented the articles of faith to the Neuendorf congregation for the sixth time. Elder Jacob Dyck did the same in Chortitza. The baptismal candidates sat on both sides of the front benches and answered the questions presented to them with a Yes! May the Lord seal this affirmation in their hearts for all eternity. Amen.

May 16

I, D. Penner and our son Diedrich made the trip to Charkov and sold our washed wool at twenty-six rubles a *pud*. We returned safely on May 30 in the evening.[3]

May 22

Elder Jacob Dyck baptized fifty-six persons of both genders in Chortitza and thirty-one persons in Neuendorf. Accept all these baptized persons into your church, O holy Jesus.

May 29

H. Penner preached the preparatory sermon in Chortitza. Prepare us all [O Lord] for holy communion.

June 2

The Claas Dycks and their daughter passed through on their way to D. Penners on the community farm.

June 5

Elder Jacob Dyck celebrated holy communion [in Chortitza] with four hundred and thirty-two members. His text was 1 Corinthians 11:23-29. Jesus accepts those sinners who acknowledge their sin from the bottom of their hearts. H. Penner presented the preparatory sermon in Neuendorf. May Your blessing rest upon it, O Lord.

June 7/8

Claas Dyck and his daughter from the community farm stopped over. They began their return journey around 12 PM. Bernard Rempel had come with them [Claas Dyck] in order to apprentice as a linen dyer with Letkemann in Halbstadt for one year. The Lord's angel accompany you.

June 10

The D. Penners from our community farm were our guests and made the return journey the next day.

June 12

In Chortitza I preached the thanksgiving sermon after holy communion on Ephesians 1:3. The Lord asked "Were not all ten cleansed? Where are the other nine?" [Luke 17:17]

Elder Jacob Dyck celebrated holy communion with three hundred and thirty-one members in Neuendorf. "The Lord is compassionate and gracious, slow to anger, abounding in love" [Psalm 103:8].

June 17

Our children, the B. Friesens, came from the community farm in order to visit us.

June 19

They [B. Friesens] left for their return journey. The Lord go with them.

In Neuendorf I preached the thanksgiving sermon after holy communion on Eph. 1:4. Jacob Regier did the same in Osterwick. Johann Penner preached in Chortitza.

June 25

The Harm Friesens stopped at our house for two hours on their way to the annual fair in Yekaterinoslav. They left after breakfast.

July 1

This morning at 12:30 AM the H. Friesens dropped by on their return journey. They left before lunch.

July 3

Jacob Regier preached in Chortitza on Matthew 10:22. Johann Penner preached in Neuendorf, Peter Dyck in Neu-Osterwick.

July 6

Peter Schmidt of Steinbach and Julius Lange son of the school teacher Wilhelm Lange of Steinbach arrived here in the evening.

July 7

They continued their journey at 6 AM. God's angel go with you dear ones.

Lehrdienst on Thursday. Gerhard Enss and P. Teigraeu appeared because of a dispute. After a long discussion the two were reconciled, as were G. Enss and Elias V. Bergen.

July 9

I preached the funeral sermon on ? for the late Peter Penner of Chortitza in the home of the bereaved. He died on July 8, 2:00 AM after an illness of one year and five months. He reached the age of fifty-four years, nine months and a few days. He was married three times. His first marriage lasted a year and a day. He sired one child, who soon died. His second marriage lasted sixteen years. He sired six children, of whom five are still alive. His third marriage lasted fifteen years and twenty-three days. He sired six children, three of whom are alive. In all he had thirteen children, five of whom died. He had twelve grandchildren, five of whom died. The Lord Jesus grant him eternal rest and a joyous resurrection with all God's children in the last days.

July 10

Elder Jacob Dyck preached in Chortitza, J. Regier in Neuendorf. God wishes to help all people come to the true knowledge of truth.

July 14

Thursday. Gerhard Penner and his wife, Abraham Dyck and his wife, and the school teacher Klippenstein appeared before the *Lehrdienst*. Dyck claimed that he had seen Penner's wife and Klippenstein in Penners' garden engaging in unmentionable acts. A sixteen-year-old girl had spread this evil rumour. At first Dyck made many excuses but finally he admitted he had seen nothing at all. He desired to clear up the matter and asked Penner and Klippenstein for forgiveness. The matter was not resolved and was referred to the brethren Johann Klassen and Jacob Friesen. If they can be reconciled by Sunday the issue will not be brought up before the *Bruederschaft*. You shall not bear false witness against your neighbour.[4]

July 17

Elder Jacob Dyck preached in Chortitza on Matthew 7:13,14. Peter Dyck preached in Neuendorf, J. Pegier in Osterwick. "Truly small is the gate and narrow the road that leads to life" [Matt. 7:14].

Abraham Dyck feigned illness and did not appear [before the *Bruederschaft*]. Young Mrs. Dyck had told Penner's chldren that their mother was a common whore. ... The matter was again referred for mediation to brother Johann Klassen and J. Friesen. Both parties will be asked to appear next Sunday. Lord have mercy and shed your grace upon us.

This afternoon our children the Friesens arrived from the community farm.

July 18

At 10 AM our children left for Rempels in Schoenhorst and then returned to their home.

July 19

I wanted to go to a funeral at the Wilhelm Dycks in Blumengart, but was unable to do so because of the unexpected arrival of the missionary ?. He came via Yekaterinoslav and stayed until 5:30 PM. I took him to ? with my wagon so that he could catch the coach. He hoped to travel via Nikolayev, Odessa, Galatz, Vienna to Basel. A truly saintly man. May God's angel go with him in all his ways and undergird him in all his endeavours. I learned so much from him. [5]

July 23

I preached the funeral sermon on ? for the departed sister Gertrude Thiessen in the home of the bereaved Franz Thiessen. She died on July 21 at 4 PM after a six-week illness at the age of seventy years, two months and fourteen days. Her first marriage lasted some nineteen years. She gave birth to four sons and six daughters. Three of her daughters died. Her second marriage of some twenty-six years produced no children. She was grandmother to sixty-five children, forty-six of whom are alive. The Lord grant her a gentle and blessed rest until that day of joyful resurrection.

July 24

I preached in Chortitza on John 1:17. Peter Dyck preached in Neuendorf, Jacob Regier in Rosengart and H. Penner in Nieder-Chortitza. Lord, revive us with your truth and grace.

Bruederschaft. The two parties (see June 14) were reconciled. Dyck admitted his wrong doing and was forgiven by the congregation and Penner. Lead us all, Lord Jesus, upon ways from which even fools cannot stray.

July 29

I preached the funeral sermon on Heb.13:14 for Friedrich, the little son of Bernd Schellenberg, in Blumengart. He died on July 27 at 3 AM after an illness of two days. He reached the age of eleven months, eight days. Blessed are the dead who die in the Lord.

Note: N. and his wife from Osterwick appeared before the *Lehrdienst* on Thursday, July 28. The couple are living in great disharmony and wish to separate. They were urged to reconcile but this proved impossible and they separated. "Watchman what is left of the night?" [Isa. 21:11].[6]

July 31

I preached in Chortitza on Isaiah 55:1-3. H. Penner preached in Neuendorf, elder Jacob Dyck in Osterwick. "Blessed are those who hunger and thirst for righteousness, for they will be filled" [Matt. 5:6].

August 7

I preached in Neuendorf on John 1:17. H. Penner preached in Chortitza "Turn to me and be saved all you ends of the earth" [Isa. 45:22].

August 14

I preached in Osterwick on Matthew 22:2-13. H. Penner preached in Chortitza, J. Penner in Neuendorf. In the afternoon D. Penner from the community farm came to visit us.

August 15

They began their return journey to the Molotschna. The Lord's angel accompany them.

August 17

State Councillor Count von Breitenbach arrived here for an inspection of the colony. He was very satisfied and left for Halbstadt on August 19. The Lord accompany them.

August 18

Thursday D. Koslowsky senior and Cornelius Vogt appeared before the *Lehrdienst* because of a quarrel about some chickens. The parties were reconciled. Similarly Gerhard Rempel and Johann Hiebert appeared because of a quarrel about some sheep and lambs. They too were reconciled and left in peace.

August 21

Johann Penner preached in Chortitza, H. Penner in Neuendorf.

In the afternoon I preached a funeral sermon on Heb. 13:14 for the four-day-old baby, J. Friesen, at the home of C. Friesen in Osterwick. "Blessed are the dead who die in the Lord" [Rev. 14:13].

Towards evening I spoke with the local mayor [of Osterwick] Gerhard Siemens at the request of elder Jacob Dyck. I pointed out the personal and eternal consequences of his heavy drinking. He promised to better himself. May God give him the strength to do so.[7]

August 25

The D. Penners and their son arrived safe and sound from the Molotschna.

August 26

At lunch, they left for the community farm. The Lord's angel accompany them.

August 28

I preached in Burwalde on Acts 24:25. Johann Penner preached in Chortitza, J. Regier in Osterwick, elder Jacob Dyck in Neuendorf. H. Penner preached at the private farm of Cornelius Friesen near the railway. Repent and be converted so that your sins be forgiven.

September 1

Elder Jacob Dyck and brother H. Penner left for Bergthal with the driver Cornelius Bergen of Chortitza. They will celebrate holy communion and preside over a deacon and ministerial election. The Lord bless this undertaking.

September 3

The teacher J. Friesen and our son Heinrich arrived here safe and sound. Thanks be to the Lord.

September 4

Peter Dyck preached in Chortitza, J. Penner in Neuendorf. Bless, Jesus, this sowing of the seed to Your glory and the salvation of the listeners.

September 5

This afternoon I and my wife, Lenchen and little Abram began our journey to the Molotschna. We spent the night at Abraham Janz's in Schoenwiese.[8]

September 6

On Tuesday 5 PM we reached the Johann Klaasens in Halbstadt where we spent the night.

September 7

This Wednesday I visited the dyer Letkemann in the district office. Then I met with G. Vogt, Johann Regier and the school teacher Gerhard Peters. For lunch we were at the widow Isbrand Friesen in Tiegenhagen and for coffeee at the widow David Wiens in Schoenau. We spent the night at the Bernd Fasts in Lichtenau.

September 8

Thursday we had lunch at Claas Hiebert's in Muensterberg and stopped for coffee at the Bernd Wiebes. We ate supper at the D. Hieberts and spent half an hour visiting the B. Niemans. We spent the night with the Claas Hieberts.

September 9

This Friday we visited at the Jacob Penners, ate lunch at the Hieberts and stopped for coffee at my sister-in-law Mrs. D. Thiessen, where we spent the night. I spent one hour with Isaac Wiens.

September 11
This Sunday we stopped for coffee at Mr. and Mrs. Cornelius Penner, where we spent the night.

September 12
We had Monday lunch at David Penner in Ohrloff and coffee at Claas Dyck. In the evening we spent two hours at the H. Heesens. For night we were at D. Penners.

September 13
On Tuesday morning we visited Peter Ens and Johann Cornies. For lunch we stopped at the Abraham Warkentins and for coffee at the Johann Doerksens. I spent one hour with the district chairperson Johann Toews. We spent the night with the H. Friesens in Tiege.

September 14
Wednesday morning we visited Johann Cornies in Ohrloff and had coffee at H. Warkentins. Then we stopped at the Claas Dyck's in Rosengart and spent the night with cousin Dyck in Neukirch.

September 15
On Thursday we had lunch with the Johann Warkentins in Prangenau. Afternoon we stopped at Peter Schmidt's in Steinbach. We had coffee with the Federaus in Elisabethal, where we spent the night.

September 16
We had Friday lunch with the Peter Schmidts in Steinbach and coffee with Friedrich Lange in the community school. Then we drove to the Johann Warkentins in Prangenau and spent the night with cousin Dirk Epp in Neukirch.

September 17
We had Saturday lunch at the Jacob Warkentins in Ladekopp. We visited the district office, then drove on to the Johann Klassens. We spent the night at the Johann Warkentins.

September 18

This Sunday I preached in the Petershagen church on Luke 19:10. We had lunch and coffee at the Johann Dycks in Ladekopp and supper at the Kroekers. We spent the night with the J. Warkentins.

September 19

We began our return journey and spent the night with Abraham Janz in Schoenwiese.

September 20

On Tuesday at 12 PM we arrived home safe and sound. Thanks to the Lord for his fatherly guidance and gracious protection.

Some Observations About the Molotschna Trip

There is certainly no inner peace in the churches. Elder B. Wedel is the shepherd of two members! There is considerable unrest in both the Rudnerweide and Gnadenfeld congregations. Fast's and Warkentin's congregations are still not working together for the common good.[9] The lively trade in wheat is momentarily curtailing the spiritual and political disputes. The Agricultural Society (*Landwirtschaftlicher Verein*) is not as strict with planting as previously. The behaviour of Johann Cornies is more despotic than Christian. The chief curator General von Insov has sent a letter requesting the members of the district office to allow the elders to remain in their posts for another three years so that the situation in the congregations may calm down. The construction of the Ohrloff church is also causing problems because the project is very costly. The Ohroff school under Heinrich Heese is doing well. Another school has been built at Steinbach where the minister Friedrich Lange is the teacher. The grain harvest is very abundant. …

Note: On September 11 Peter Dyck preached in Chortitza, Jacob Regier in Neuendorf and Johann Penner in Osterwick.

September 18

J. Regier preached in Chortitza, H. Penner in Neuendorf. The Lord is near to them who call upon Him.

Note: H. Penner preached the preparatory sermon on September 4 in Bergthal. On Wednesday September 7 elder Jacob Dyck celebrated holy communion with the congregation. Deacon and ministerial elections were held in the afternoon. Klippenstein and Bernd Friesen were elected as deacons, Jacob Neufeld as minister. The Lord be his strength. May he lead them on the right pathway. The minister Jacob Braun was invested with all spiritual functions except baptism and communion. The Lord be his helper and fill him with power from on high. Elder Jacob Dyck and brother H. Penner returned safe and sound on September 9. Praise God!

September 22

Agatha Peters of Neuendorf appeared before the *Lehrdienst* on Thursday. She had an affair with the blacksmith Peter Wiebe's apprentice, a Lutheran. She expressed regret and promised to break off with him. The matter was referred to the *Bruederschaft* on Sunday.

The wife of Aron Peters of Blumengart left him on account of physical abuse. Peters promised to improve and both were reconciled. May the reconciliation last.

Yesterday elder Jacob Warkentin of Altonau and deacon Johann Klassen of Ohrloff arrived at the residence of elder Jacob Dyck. Why? They plan to leave today. The Lord's angel go with them.

September 25

I preached in Neuendorf on Isaiah 55: 1-3. Elder Jacob Dyck preached in Chortitza, Peter Dyck in Osterwick. O Lord Jesus, satisfy my poor soul with the water of life.

Bruederschaft. Agatha Peters was excommunicated from the congregation. O Lord have mercy on us.

Note: On September 23 a widow, Mrs. Peter Enss, arrived from Heubuden in Prussia with her children. There was also a Mierau, his wife and their children Peter and Anna. They rested until Sunday and left for the Molotschna after church. Dear ones, may the Lord guide you.

October 2

Elder Jacob Dyck preached the harvest and thanksgiving sermon in Chortitza. H. Penner preached in Neuendorf.

October 7

My brother-in-law Peter Loewen of Altonau and their children

Peter and Agata arrived at our house while Isaak Wiens of Altonau arrived in Einlage. We want to divide the inheritance of our dear grandfather. I contacted my brother-in-law H. Thiessen in Yekaterinoslav in this regard.

October 9

I preached in Neuendorf, H. Penner in Neu-Osterwick. Seek out those who are lost, Lord Jesus. You took on human form for this.

Bruederschaft Agatha Peters was accepted into the congregation by elder Jacob Dyck. Luke 15 (parable of the lost son).

In the afternoon Peter Loewens left for Neuendorf to visit their friends. In the evening the H. Thiessens and their daughter Catarina arrived from Yekaterinoslav and stayed with the Dycks.

October 10

This morning Peter Loewens returned from Neuendorf.

October 11

I presided at the marriage of Carl Grunau and Maria Enss at the home of Johannes Enss in Burwalde. May the Lord's blessing rest upon this pair…

October 12

The estate of our blessed grandfather H. Thiessen was sold through public auction to the highest bidder. The capital amounted to one thousand and sixty-four rubles and fifty eight kopecks per family (there were five families). One thousand and fifty-five rubles are deposited with Johann Klassen in Halbstadt and are not included in this sum. The Wiens spent the night at our house.

October 13

This morning at 5:30 AM our daughter, Mrs. Friesen, gave birth to a healthy daughter, Helena. May Holy Jesus grant them peace and love.

The Johann Dycks from Ladekopp were with us for lunch, then went to visit H. Schwarz. Peter Loewens left here at 2:30 PM after we had coffee together. Then Johann Dycks dropped by again. In the morning the H. Thiessens left for Ekaternisolav. The Lord's angel accompany you dear ones.

October 16

I preached in Chortitza on I John 4:19. Elder Jacob Dyck preached in Neuendorf, Johann Penner in Einlage. Love conquers death.

October 18

I preached the funeral sermon on ? for Catarina, the daughter of Cornelius Friesen in Osterwick. She died during the night of October 14-15, with only her Saviour in attendance. She reached the age of four years, eight months and twenty-seven days. Let the little children come unto me.

October 21

I preached the funeral sermon on ? for the departed sister Sara Klassen Blumengart in the home of Isaak Klassen. She died on October 19 at 3 AM at the age of twenty-eight years and ten months. She was married for ten years and ten months. She gave birth to four sons and two daughters. Three of her sons preceeded her into eternity. She was ill for ten weeks. May Holy Jesus grant her a serene and blessed rest.

October 23

I preached in Neuendorf on Matthew 6:13. H. Penner preached in Chortitza, Johann Penner in Osterwick.

October 28

Gerhard Wiens from Steinbach spent the night with us. He, together with the teacher for Russian language in the Steinbach school, left on October 29. May the Lord's angel accompany you dear friends.

October 30

H. Penner preached in Chortitza on Jeremiah 31:3, Johann Penner in Neuendorf. Love is the fulfillment of the law.

Bruederschaft. Mrs. H. Dyck of Neuendorf, who was married two months ago, confessed that she had had an affair with the son of Peter Dyck both before and after her baptism. She was excommunicated from the church. Lord have mercy on all!

November 6

I preached in Osterwick on John 1:17. H Penner preached in Neuendorf, Johann Penner in Chortitza. After the sermon he presided at the marriage of Johann Enss from Rosenthal and ? . The Lord bless them to His honour and glory.

November 10

I presided at the marriage of Cornelius Pauls and Margaretha Siemens at the home of the elder Jacob Dyck in Rosenthal.

November 12

I and Dirk [Diedrich] travelled to Yekaterinoslav along very bad roads. We arrived at 7 PM.

November 13

Brother Johann Penner preached in Chortitza, H. Penner in Neuendorf. May the Lord bless the sowing of the seed.

November 14

We arrived home safely. Thank God.

November 15

I presided at the marriage of Isaac Enss and Helena Enss at the Schoenhorst residence of Cornelius Enss. The steppe was a sheet of ice.

November 20

Peter Dyck preached in Chortitza on Matthew 4:13,14. Johann Penner in Neuendorf, H. Penner in Neu-Osterwick.

November 21

I and our children Diedrich, Heinrich and Helena travelled to H. Thiessens in Yekaterinoslav for a wedding. The roads were in poor condition.

November 22

I presided at the Yekaterinoslav marriage of Abraham Krahn and Catarina Thiessen. Lead this young pair on the correct pathway, Lord Jesus. The weather was stormy but we arrived home that evening safe and sound. Thank the Lord for His grace.

November 27

Peter Dyck preached in Chortitza, Jacob Regier in Neuendorf. Prepare our hearts for your service Lord Jesus.

December 4

J. Regier preached in Chortitza on Rom. 13:11-14. Peter Dyck preached in Neuendorf, Johann Penner in Osterwick, elder Jacob Dyck in Nieder Chortitza. "Arise, shine for your light has come" [Isa. 60:1].

December 6

I presided at the marriage of Isaac Friesen and Susanna Duerksen at the Schoeneberg residence of David Doerksen. Guide this couple in Your ways.

December 8

I presided at the marriage of Abraham Friesen and Catarina Schwarz at the Nieder Chortitza residence af Abraham Hiebert. Be with them, O Lord Jesus.

December 11

I preached in Neuendorf on Psalm 24:9-11; J. Regier preached in Chortitza. May the Lord prepare our hearts.

December 15

Thursday. Three youths from ? and three youths from Osterwick were ordered to appear before the *Lehrdienst* on complaint of Peter Dyck of Kronsthal. When Dyck held services at his house they engaged in all sorts of mischief.[10] Dyck's warnings were of no avail and they began to call him names, even on the street. Following a discussion they promised to behave and were reconciled with Dyck. Let's hope they keep their promise.

Isaac Klassen from ? complained that his mother-in-law told him that his dying wife had accused him of secretly carrying on with Mrs. Heinrich Friesen. Mrs. Cornelius de Veer also claimed this was true. Since there were no eyewitnesses the parties concerned were reconciled and went home. "Though you grind a fool in a mortar . . . you will not remove his folly from him" [Prov. 27:22]. How true!

December 16

The *Lehrdienst* met at the residence of elder Jacob Dyck together with members of the district office and the orphan administration [*Waisenamt*]. The problem: Dyck had been elected to head the *Waisenamt* by majority vote, but did not wish to have the office. Finally after much persuasion he accepted it for another three years.

It was decided that the annual taxes, ten percent of the capital and interest where applicable, must be paid when due. If a debtor cannot pay, the district office will, in public auction, sell such goods as are necessary to cover the debt. . . .

December 18

On this second advent Sunday elder Jacob Dyck preached in Chortitza on Luke 21:25-36. Brother J. Regier preached in Neuendorf. P. Dyck in Osterwick. Lord Jesus be our refuge in time of need.

Decmber 19

At 8 AM I and my dear wife left for Yekaterinoslav to visit our brother-in-law H. Thiessen. We arrived at 3:30 PM. He had left for Molotschna.

December 22

We left Yekaterinoslav at 8 AM and met H. Thiessen on his return journey. He had not stopped in Halbstadt. We arrived home safe and sound at 4 PM. Thanks to the Lord for his guidance and protection.

December 25

On Sunday, the first day of Christmas, I preached in Osterwick on John 1:14. Elder Jacob Dyck preached in Chortitza on Luke 2:15-20, J. Regier in Neuendorf, Peter Dyck in Schoenhorst, H. Penner in Burwalde, Johann Penner in Einlage.

December 26

On the second day of Christmas I preached in Chortitza on Isaiah 9:6. Elder Jacob Dyck preached in Neuendorf, Peter Dyck in Osterwick. Come Lord Jesus enter all our hearts.

Some Observations on 1838

In the past year one hundred and thirty-five females and one hundred and thirty-five males were born, a total of two hundred and seventy. Thirty men and thirty-nine women died, a total of sixty-nine. Fifty-one couples were married (in both congregations).

Weather. During the past winter we experienced heavy frost and little snow. The spring was cold. There was much rain during the summer as well as the fall. Until now the winter has been mild. There have been good sleigh tracks. Winter began in mid-November.

Harvest. The hay was of poor quality and there was little of it. The summer fallow had a lot of weeds. The winter rye was poor. The spring grains were generally good as were the vegetable gardens. The winter rye germinated well this fall.

Public Health. There were few fevers, but many intestinal problems. Scabies and ring worm often occurred but were not taken seriously by the patients and seldom healed. Throat infections were cured. A measles epidemic struck in November, but was contained. There was no smallpox. Cattle pest erupted in Rosenthal at the end of October and destroyed more than two-thirds of the cattle. It broke out in Chortitza at the end of December. One farmer in Schoenhorst lost almost all of his cattle to the infection. Diarrhea plagued the community sheep farm and killed many of the lambs.

Price of Wool and Grain. Wool prices: twenty-six to thirty-one rubles per *pud* for washed wool; fifteen to twenty rubles per *pud* for unwashed wool. Rye: six to seven rubles per *chetvert*. Wheat: ten to twelve rubles, buckwheat ten to eleven rubles per *chetvert*. Barley and oats: one ruble seventy-five kopecks to two rubles and twenty-five kopecks [per *chetvert*]. Millet: four to five rubles per *chetvert*. . . .

Thanks to the Lord's blessing the prosperity of the farmers has noticeably increased. Many new houses are being built and there is increased luxury. No thefts were reported. A few cases of fornication and adultery were confessed thanks to the pangs of conscience. The profligacy of youth intensifies as does the drinking—no, guzzling—of liquor and the dancing at weddings. Love has grown cold in many. Few measures have been taken to curb these excesses and many are ignoring them. Apparent peace still reigns in the congregation—but the slightest spark could ignite a conflagration that could consume it.

In October 1837, the Molotschna congregations presented a petition to his majesty Nicholas I in the Crimea regarding the confirmation of the *Privilegium*. It was signed by elders Bernard Fast, Bejamin Ratzlaff, Benjamin Wedel and Wilhelm Lange, the district officials Vogt and Johann Regier . . . and Johann Kornies and Gerhard Enss.

The answer arrived this December and as I see it, contained a full affirmation of the *Privilegium*. Elder Jacob Dyck was incensed since the petition was handed in without the approval of elder Jacob Warkentin. He wrote to Warkentin and both were inclined to complain to the Guardian Committee [*Comitaet*] about the action of the other elders. They claimed his majesty and the ministry were insulted by the petition. It's so sad when premature judgement, hate, partisan politics, and ignorance rule. How unwise it would be if a complaint were sent to the Guardian Committee.

O my God, make things right. Quench the rising flame of discontent and instil love and trust towards You and the neighbour in all our hearts. The seed of discontent is being sown in our and in the Molotschna congregations and it is spreading like an obnoxious weed threatening to devour the good seed which, praise God, has been sown.

The kingdom of peace and the kingdom of Jesus will soon emerge in blessing and power. Hallelujah.

Endnotes

[1] The reader may wonder whether the cases of adultery and fornication mentioned in Epp's diary represent the tip of the iceberg. This is probably not the case. The community was relatively small and villagers knew a great deal about one another. Affairs were difficult to conceal and invariably came to public notice. In all likelihood there was another dynamic at work. The Russian Mennonites of the mid-nineteenth century appear to have a well trained sense of public morality. At times the promptings of personal conscience led to confession and the accompanying public discipline and restoration. In other instances, as the diary amply illustrates, excommunication accomplished the same result.

[2] In David Epp's estimation alcohol abuse was a serious problem in the community. Beer brewing and the distilling of liquor were considered rather normal occupations in the Prussian Mennonite tradition.These rights were among the privileges granted to the new immigrants by Russian authorities. In a setting where wine and beer consumption were culturally accepted, a segment of the population was always subject to alcoholism. Furthermore the presence of a pub in many larger villages as well as the ready availability of vodka or an equivalent liquor from Russian sources compounded the problem. While it was quite normal to attend the annual fairs in the larger Ukrainian cities, the setting proved problematic for some of the village lads. When they were forced to appear before the *Lehrdienst*, it did not much matter whether their actions were intended to mark a coming of age or a proof of manliness. A more serious issue, of course, related to the violence associated with drunkenness. Discipline by the community was, in Epp's opinion, the only way to deal with the problem.

[3] Epp's reference to the sale of wool in Charkov graphically illustrates the vast distance from markets, which significantly crippled the early economic development of the Chortitza settlement.

[4] Gossip and rumour were everyday realities in Mennonite village life. Slander, as recorded in this entry, seriously damaged one's public reputation. On the other hand, appearing before the *Bruederschaft* would be even more humiliating for the perpetrators.

[5] Epp's spiritual concerns naturally focussed on the community he knew and loved. Personally he seems to have gotten an occasional glimpse into the larger Christian world, whether through a missionary or Bible salesperson.

[6] This is one of the rare cases of actual marital separation cited in the diary, though there are references to marital disputes, abuse and dysfunctional families (see September 22, 1838).

[7] Epp does not make many references to his personal pastoral work since in part such activity was done in partnership with other individuals in the *Lehrdienst*. In this instance, confronting a powerful individual like the Osterwick mayor must have taken considerable courage.

[8] David Epp's periodic journeys to the Molotschna illustrate something of the dynamic of Russian Mennonite society. Strategically placed friends and relatives provided overnight accommodation or daytime drink and sustenance as the

travellers went from house to house and village to village.

[9] For an explanation of these quarrels see the introductory comments.

[10] David Epp's reference to house services possibly relates to a situation in which corporate worship services were only held in three locations on a weekly basis—Chortitza, Osterwick and Neuendorf. Serious Christians in small villages like Kronsthal obviously gathered in homes from time to time. In the mid-1850s, when revival began in the Chortitza colony, a number of such "house churches" emerged.

1839

January 1

"Christ is all and is in all" [Col. 3:11]. In the holy and sweet name of Jesus who is God over all, praised in all eternity, from whom comes all our help. Amen.

Through your precious blood, Lord Jesus Christ, grant us new courage based on our steadfast faith and corresponding actions. May our every activity from beginning to end be a blessing.

Lord our Saviour, you feed your hungry people in the desert with heavenly manna and let fall the dew of Hermon on the mountains of Zion [Psa. 133:3] and promise blessing and life now and for evermore. More refreshing than the dew of Hermon or Zion's heights and more precious than the Manna in the wilderness, is the word of Your mouth, the Gospel, you eternal merciful God. Speak to us during this year. Make your Word a refreshing, nurturing, transforming life force in our hearts for teaching, rebuking and correcting in righteousness [2 Tim. 3:16] Amen.

On this day I preached in the school on the Island of Chortitza on Ephesians 4: 22-24. Elder Jacob Dyck preached in Chortitza, J. Regier in New-Osterwick, H. Penner in Neuendorf, P. Dyck in Schoenhorst and Johann Penner in Burwalde. O Lord Jesus, give us new strength and new life through your grace.

January 5

Today brother Jacob Braun from Bergthal arrived at Abraham S.'s. J.B. visited with us for several hours in the afternoon.

January 6

Elder Jacob Dyck preached in Chortitza on the Feast of Epiphany. His text was Matthew 2:1-13. Peter Dyck spoke in Neuendorf, J. Regier in Osterwick. "Arise and shine O my soul for your light is come." [Isa. 60:1]

January 8

H. Penner preached in Chortitza; elder J. Dyck preached in Neuendorf. The Lord be with us all.

January 10

I presided at the marriage of Abraham Friesen and Helena Thiessen at the Wilhelm Friesen residence in New Osterwick. Lead them with your counsel and graciously accept them.

January 12

In the afternoon I began a trip to the Molotschna. Accompanying me were our children Jacob and Heinrich, Bernard Rempel my son-in-law and a young man Johann Braun. We drove a wagon even though conditions were right for sleighing. We spent the night at K. in Schoenwiese. We continued our journey at 3 AM. The road was rough and some snow fell. We spent the night in Gruenthal.

January 14

Severe snow drifting in the morning; by noon it was raining. At 11 AM we arrived at John Klassens in Halbstadt. Here my travelling companions took their leave.

January 15

Frostbite on one of my toes kept me from going to church. I had coffee with sister Claas Hiebert in Muensterberg, where I also had my accommodation for the night.

January 16

I had coffee with my sister-in-law Mrs. Dietrich Thiessen as well as at the Loewens'.

January 17 - January 24[1]

In the morning I visited elder Jacob Warkentin, in the afternoon Mrs. Cornelius Penner. My night accommodation was with my sister-in-law. I boarded one of my three horses here and drove the other two to Ohrloff, where my cousin David Penner lives. Then I visited Class Dyck and in the evening dropped in at H. Heese, Johann Cornies and the venerable Peter Enss. I slept at the home of the H. Friesens. I had coffee with the district chairperson Toews in Tiege. Dietrich Hiebert lives here as well.

A rapid thaw began and I had to drive through water between Lichtfelde and Neukirch. I spent the night at my cousin D. Epp's. I visited my brother-in-law Johann Warkentin who is suffering from a severe urinary disorder. My night lodging was at D.E. Next day [January 24] I and little Henry drove to Peter Schmidt in Steinbach, where I left Heinrich with the teachers Lange and Friesen so that he can learn German and Russian. Mrs. Schmidt will take the place of his mother.

Dear Lord Jesus, I give my son over to you. You will be a mother and father to him. Protect his youthful heart from all sin. Give him a love of learning. Enlighten his mind that he may delight in Your Word, which shall be a light and a lamp on his pathway. Give him an obedient, compliant heart, which will enable him to follow You in all his ways. Amen.

Each day there will be four hours of instruction in German and four hours of instruction in Russian. The cost is three rubles per month.

In the evening elder Friedrich Lange from Gnadenfeld came to Peter Schmidt and spent the night.

January 25

I travelled to Altonau with Peter Schmidt, his wife and children as well as the elder and teacher Lange. It was the funeral of the widow Claas Wiens who had died at the home of her daughter, Mrs. Toews. I said goodbye to Mr. Friesen and our Henry and began my return journey. I bade farewell to the Johann Warkentins in Prangenau. I ate lunch at the D. Epps in Neukirch.

January 27

On Friday noon I and Jacob, who had partially recovered from the measles, drove to Blumenort to the H. Friesens. Their children were sick with the measles. I left Jacob there.

January 28

After a night's lodging at the W. Warkentins in Tiege I visited Claas Dyck in Rosenort, had coffee with the H. Friesens in Blumenort and lunch with Abraham Warkentin. I called on David Penner and met Jacob here. I stopped at Johann Cornies' residence but he was not at home. Then I went back to Claas Dyck.

January 29

I spent the night at D. Penner, but did not go to church. During the afternoon I visited with my sister-in-law Mrs. D. Thiessen in Altonau. In the evening I dropped in on Gerhard Enss. I took my night's lodging at the Thiessens.

January 30

I said goodbye to the Thiessens and Loewens as well as to the C. Penners. I stopped for coffee at the Claas Hieberts in Muensterberg. I spent the night at the Bernd Fasts in Lichtenau.

January 31

I drove on to Jacob Martens in Tiegenhagen. Later, I had lunch with Johann Klassen in Halbstadt. In the afternoon I spent an hour and a half with the secretary Johann Regier in the district office.

February 1

We left the Johann Klassens in Halbstadt at 7 AM. My travel companions were my son Jacob, Christian Hamm and his son Martin from Chortitza, as well as a young Rempel who was visiting from Prussia. The road was very rough. We arrived at the home of Peter Krahn in Schoenwiese at 5.30 PM and spent the night. Mrs. Krahn had been bed-ridden for three weeks with a sprained ankle. Abraham Krahn and his wife had journeyed to Yekaterinoslav to visit the H. Thiessens.

February 2

We arrived home safe and sound at noon. A thousand thanks to the Lord for his gracious guidance and protection. Amen. At home I found Lenchen and Abram sick with the measles. Johann and Annie have almost recovered.

Some Observations about the Visit to the Molotschna

The road to the Molotschna was very bumpy and hard. There was almost no snow and seventeen degrees of frost. Then came the heavy rains which caused a great deal of damage to structures, roads, bridges and dams as well as hay and straw stacks. Two people, a Russian and a Nogier, were drowned in the flood waters. The return journey was also very bumpy.

The Ohrloff school with the teacher Heese is doing well. The Steinbach school is doing very well. The teacher Friedrich Lange has forty students in the German language program; Johann Friesen has twenty students in the Russian language program. The Lord will bless this institution, which was erected to his glory.

A new leaven has been mixed into the flour and new unrest is fomenting. In October, 1837, a petition was presented to his royal majesty Nicholas I in the Crimea requesting a confirmation of the Mennonite privileges granted by Paul I.[2] It was presented by elder Fast, elder Lange and Johann Cornies. Elder Jacob Warkentin and his church feel that the response gives cause for alarm. They believe his majesty was offended by the petition. They claim the petitioners did not consult with the Chortitza churches or with Warkentine's church. Jealousy is the root of all evil.

Peace nourishes, discord destroys.

The other issue relates to Christmas. In order to please the children the teachers in some schools erected a Christmas tree. When the gifts were being distributed they explained the purpose of the celebration by telling the story of Jesus' birth as recorded in Scripture. Some say it amounts to image worship, apostasy and the like. As long as there is no inner renewal there will be no peace in our society. The attempt of the district office to diffuse the unrest by all kinds of activities will fail. When will we truly be satisfied and find our desired happiness....

February 5

Elder Jacob Dyck celebrated holy communion with one hundred and eighty-six members in Chortitza. I could not attend on account of my bad foot. J. Regier preached the preparatory sermon in Neuendorf. "Behold, I stand at the door and knock, if anyone hears my voice and opens the door I will go in..." [Rev. 3:20].

February 7

I heard in passing that elder Jacob Dyck and H. Penner left for the Molotschna to visit elder J. Warkentin. It probably concerns the petition which the four Molotschna elders gave to his majesty in the Crimea in 1837. Complaints about this will reach the Guardians Committee. It is not going to end well.

February 8

Today Jacob Regier told me that elder Jacob Hildebrand from the Island of Chortitza also joined the party visiting elder Jacob Warkentin.

February 9

I presided at the marriage of Jacob Paetkau and Margareta Dyck in the home of the widow Johann Dyck in Chortitza. O Lord Jesus, grant this young couple your blessing.

February 12

I preached in Neuendorf on Acts 10:34. We were unable to celebrate communion since elder Jacob Dyck had not yet returned from the Molotschna. The congregation was invited to celebrate next Sunday. You Lord are my help in need. In Chortitza the sermon of Thanksgiving was preached by Johann Penner. Elder Jacob Dyck and H. Penner returned from the Molotschna at 9 PM.

February 13

I preached the funeral sermon for Jacob Dyck's son Franz. He died after a thirteen-day illness with measles at the age of one year, eight months and eight days.

February 14

I preached the funeral sermon on ? for the departed sister Agatha

Hiebert of Einlage in the home of the miller Johann Hiebert. She died on Thursday, February 9, at 2 PM after a thirty-eight week illness. She reached the age of sixty-one years, seven days. Her first marriage lasted nineteen years. She bore three children, two of whom died. Her second marriage lasted twenty-six years, nine months and three days. She had three more children, but only one survived. In all she had six children. Her six grandchildren are all alive. Rest sweetly, dear sister, after your long suffering. Your soul is in Jesus' bosom.

February 16

I preached the funeral sermon on ? for the young son of our neighbour Bernd Rempel and the son of his renter, a Catholic named M. Kornat. The first child died on February 12 at 4 PM following a thirteen-day illness. He was thirty-eight weeks old. His name was John. The second child, Martin, died on February 11 at 3:30 PM following a fourteen day-illness. He was three and a half years old. Blessed are those who die in the Lord.

February 18

Elder Jacob Hildebrand and his wife visited us.

February 19

Elder Jacob Dyck celebrated holy communion in Neuendorf with two hundred and thirty-one members of the congregation. I, unworthy as I am, and my dear wife were also present at the table of the Lord. O Lord Jesus, heal me and all those of broken heart.

Johann Penner preached in Chortitza. O Lord, bless his words to the hearts of his listeners.

February 20

I learned that elder Jacob Dyck wants to object to the petition presented to his majesty by the Molotschna elders, which called for the reaffirmation of our *Privilegium*. Jealousy and fanaticism, not brotherly love, are at the root of this action. May the Lord in His grace ward off a calamity.

February 26

I preached in Chortitza on Isaiah 53:4. The thanksgiving sermon after holy communion was preached by H. Penner in Neuendorf. J. Regier preached in Osterwick. Let your suffering and pain always remain in my thoughts.

March 2

The widow of Abraham Neufeld of Kronswide was invited to appear before the *Lehrdienst* on account of her dissolute lifestyle. She did not come. She was ordered to appear on Sunday. In the afternoon we examined the *Privilegium*, which had not been done for two years. It was in excellent condition, undamaged by moisture or mould.

March 4

I preached the funeral sermon on Psalm 39: 5-6 for David Hamm's son Gerhard. He died on February 28 at ? AM after a nineteen-day illness. He was four years, eight months and five days old. Lord, help us to remember that we must die.

March 5

I preached in Chortitza on Luke 22:39-44. Peter Dyck preached in Neuendorf. God be merciful to me a sinner.

Bruederschaft. David Paetkau committed incest with his stepdaughters. He and the oldest, a Mrs. Baerg, were excommunicated from the congregation. The youngest daughter, who is not yet baptized, has given birth to a son. Similarly, S.K., who on his own admission committed sodomy, was also expelled. Mrs. Neufeld sent word that she was sick. She was ordered to appear before the congregation next Sunday. "What does it profit a person if they win the whole world…"[Mark 8:36].

March 7

I preached the funeral sermon on ? for the young child Peter Martens, the son of Jacob Martens of Berthal. The funeral was held in the home of David Hamm in Chortitza. He died on Sunday at 1 PM after an illness of thirteen days. He was about two years of age. Of such are the kingdom of God.

March 11

I preached the funeral sermon on ? for Margaretha Epp, the daughter of Peter Epp, Chortitza. She was ill for fourteen days. She died on

Tuesday at 10 AM at the age of one year, two months and twenty-seven days. We also buried the daughter of the tenant [*Einwohner*] Elisabeth Lindenau. She was sick for ten days and died on Monday at 6.30 PM at the age of one year, three months and twenty-four days. "The body that is sown is perishable, it is resurrected imperishable." [1 Cor. 15:42]

March 12

I preached in Neuendorf on Isaiah 53:7. Brother Peter Dyck preached in Chortitza, J. Penner in Osterwick. Lord, allow your bitter suffering to benefit me always. Help me to purge my thoughts of sin, which always plague me. Help me to remember what it cost you to redeem me.

Bruederschaft. Dirk Rempel and Wilhelm Friesen of Schoenhorst secretly obtained liquor in Michailovka. The issue was discussed by the brethren. After many apologies the matter was dropped. They were instructed to clarify the issue with the tenant of the distillery. The widow, Mrs. Abraham Neufeld, did not make an appearance and on account of her disobedience was excommunicated from the congregation.

Julius Klassen of Burwalde and the Wiebes from Nieder-Chortitza were accepted as congregation members by elder Jacob Dyck. Jesus accepts sinners.

March 13

Brother Peter Schmidt from Steinbach stopped here for the night on his return journey from Yekaterinoslav. Our son Heinrich who is boarding with them has recovered from the measles and is well. Praise and thanks be to the dear Saviour for ever.

March 14

Brother Schmidt continued his journey this morning. The Lord's angel keep watch over him. In the afternoon I preached the funeral sermon on Hebrews 13:14 for Maria, the daughter of the tenant [*Einwohner*] Kornat. She died after a six-week illness on March 11 at 2 AM. She was about a year old. Jesus accepts the little children.

March 19

Palm Sunday. J. Regier preached in Chortitza on Matthew 21:1-9. Peter Dyck preached in Neuendorf.

March 24

Good Friday. I preached in Osterwick on John 19:28-33. Elder Jacob Dyck preached in Chortitza, J. Regier in Neuendorf. Dear Lord, grant this poor sinner grace to bury his past sins and walk with me in a new life of the Spirit.

March 26

Easter. Elder Jacob Dyck spoke in Chortitza on the first day of Easter. I preached in Burwalde on Mark 16:1-8. J. Regier preached in Osterwick, H. Penner in Neuendorf and P. Dyck in Schoenhorst. Arise anew in us, Lord Jesus, as you arose from the dead.

March 27

The second day of Easter. I preached in Chortitza on ? . Elder J. Dyck preached in Osterwick and P. Dyck preached in Neuendorf. Peace be with you. With these words risen Lord you call your disciples. Grant your peace to my own poor heart.

My sister Anna Epp has been in bed since mid-November, but her body is healthy. She has great doubts about her soul's salvation. At one point she thought she saw Satan coming to get her soul. Such trials are so difficult. You who suffered in Gethsemane, help.[3]

March 29

I preached the funeral sermon on ? at the Heinrich Hildebrand residence in Burwalde. Their little son Gerhard died on the first day of Easter at 4:30 PM following a severe four-day illness. He reached the age of two years, ten months and twenty-four days. Let the little children come to me and don't hinder them for of such is the kingdom of God [Luke 18:16].

April 2

Elder Jacob Dyck presented the articles of faith to the Chortitza congregation. I did the same in Neuendorf. The church in Neuendorf prayed for the sick sister Thiessen of Schoenhorst. The Lord's will be done.

April 5

I preached a funeral sermon on ? for the departed sister Anna Thiessen at the Schoenhorst home of Elias Baergen. She died on April

3 at 4:30 PM in her forty-sixth year. She was married for some twenty-five years and gave birth to nine children, four of whom died. The Lord grant her a gentle rest and a joyous resurrection.

April 6

I preached the funeral sermon on Psalm 39:5-6 for little Johann, the son of Cornelius Epp of Rosengart. He died on April 3 at 12 PM following a seventeen-day illness. He reached the age of two years and one day. Jesus receives the children.

The *Lehrdienst* met on Thursday morning. The issue involved Abraham Kroeger from Rosenthal and Johann E. The latter had appropriated a cow hide belonging to the community and sold it. When the cows returned home [from the community pasture], he also appropriated Kroeger's cow. Public pressure forced him to return the cow, but then he claimed he had given Kroeger the cow as a gift. He finally admitted the cow belonged to Kroeger and both were reconciled. You can slap a fool in the face but he will not leave his foolishness.

April 7

I preached the funeral sermon for the departed sister Justina Rempel of Einlage in the home of Abraham Froese. She died on April 3 at 11 AM after a three-week illness at the age of fifty-eight years, seven months and five days. She was married some twenty-four years and had twelve children, eight of whom died. She had four grandchildren, two of whom died.

April 9

In Chortitza Elder Jacob Dyck read the articles of faith for a second time. I did the same thing in Neuendorf. Believe on the Lord Jesus and you will be saved.

Bruederschaft in Chortitza. David Paetkau showed true repentance and was accepted into the congregation by elder Jacob Dyck. Dirk Rempel and Wilhelm Friesen were excommunicated from the congregation on account of drunkenness and fighting.

April 13

On Thursday Jacob Olfert from Schoenhorst appeared before the *Lehrdienst*. In the afternoon I preached a funeral sermon at the

Neuendorf residence of Peter Reimer for the young Anganeta Friesen. She died after a four-week illness on April 10 at 8 AM at the age of three years, six months and sixteen days.

April 16

I presented the articles of faith to the congregation in Neuendorf for the third time while elder J. Dyck did the same in Chortitza. There were sixty-nine baptismal candidates of both genders, but three were not accepted. Who believes and is baptized will be saved. Who does not believe will be condemned [Mark 16:16].

Bruederschaft. Wilhelm Friesen from Schoenhorst was accepted as a member of the congregation by elder J. Dyck. Grant him true repentance O Lord.

April 20

This morning our son Heinrich arrived safe and sound from the school in Steinbach. The Lord Jesus be thanked for his gracious protection. He was there for three months less five days.

April 23

I presented the articles of faith to the Neuendorf congregation for the fourth time. Elder J. Dyck did the same in Chortitza. There are nineteen male and fourteen female baptismal candidates in Neuendorf—thirty-three in all. How shall a young man keep his way pure? [Psalm 119:9]... Wallmann, who had an affair with the daughter of Jacob Dyck of Rosengart (she gave birth to a child), was excommunicated from the congregation.

April 30

I presented the articles of faith to the Neuendorf congregation for the fifth time, while elder Jacob Dyck did so in Chortitza. In Neuendorf there are nineteen male and thirteen female candidates. In Chortitza there are seventy-five of both genders—in all one hundred and seven. In Neuendorf the daughter of Johann Peters from Kronsweide had no *Steller* [advocate]. No one knew why and so her name was dropped from the list.

Elder Jacob Dyck warned the brethren against liquor smugglers. Those who are caught will be dealt with according to community regulations and we desire the authorities to enforce them. The congregation [in Neuendorf] gave its approval. Chortitza agreed to take a similar course of action.

Elder Jacob Dyck, supported by H. Penner, declared that the girls shall not wear their braids on the side of their heads. The young men are not to let their hair grow long over their foreheads. This is vanity.

Dirk Rempel Senior from Schoenhorst was accepted as a member of the congregation by elder J. Dyck. The congregation was also admonished to refrain from drinking strong liquor. May the Lord bless these admonitions. In the evening Claas Dyck from Rosengart and his friend Eduard came to spend the night.

May 1

This morning they [Claas and Eduard?] left for the community sheep farm.

May 2

Elder Jacob Dyck examined the baptismal candidates in the Chortitza church. Give strength, O Jesus, where strength is lacking. In the afternoon I presided at the wedding of the widower J. Hiebert and the widow Elisabeth Friesen in Einlage. Guide this couple, O Holy Jesus.

May 4

Ascension Day. I preached in Neuendorf on Mark 16:19-20 and examined the thirty-two baptismal candidates. In Chortitza elder Jacob Dyck preached on the theme: "Our walk is in Heaven" and examined the baptismal candidates on the second half of the catechism.

May 7

In Chortitza elder Jacob Dyck presented the articles of faith for the sixth time. The young people (baptismal candidates) were asked the customary questions. Oh Lord Jesus be our yea and amen.

May 11

The children of the H. Thiessens, Heinrich and Mariechen, left for the Molotschna.

May 13

Our children B. Friesens, who live on the community sheep farm, came for a visit.

May 14

On this first day of Pentecost elder Jacob Dyck preached on John 3:16-21. Jacob Braun from Bergthal, who arrived here yesterday with his wife and children, preached in Neuendorf. H. Penner preached in Schoenhorst, Jacob Regier in Osterwick. Come Father, Son and Holy Spirit, and dwell with us.

May 15

On the second day of Pentecost elder Jacob Dyck baptized seventy-five persons of both genders from Chortitza and twelve from Bergthal—eighty-seven persons in all. Our son Jacob was among them. Baptize him my Saviour with the Holy Spirit and with fire [Luke 3:16]. Wallmann was accepted as a member of the congregation by elder Jacob Dyck. May his repentance be genuine.

I presented the articles of faith to the Neuendorf congregation for the sixth time and directed the customary questions to the baptismal candidates. May their hearts be in a correct state.

In the afternoon our children the Friesens left for Schoenhorst. Tomorrow they return to the community sheep farm. The Lord go with them.

May 18

I and our son David left for Yekaterinoslav on business and returned in the evening safe and sound. Thanks be to the Saviour for his gracious protection.

May 20

This morning Claas Dyck from Rosengart and his friend Eduard stopped by on their return trip from Charkov. They fed their horses for an hour and then returned home. The Lord go with you.

May 27

Brother J. Braun and his wife from Bergthal visited us in the afternoon.

May 28

Elder Jacob Dyck celebrated holy communion in the Chortitza church with four hundred and seventy-eight persons of both genders. The ministers Jacob Braun and Johann Neufeld from the Bergthal settlement were also here for holy communion. Heal us all, O Lord Jesus, for we are ill. Brother Heinrich Penner preached the preparatory sermon in Neuendorf.

June 4

I preached the sermon of Thanksgiving in Chortitza on Ephesians 1:3. In Neuendorf elder Jacob Dyck celebrated holy communion with two hundred and eighty-two members. Thanks to Holy Jesus for all his benefits.

June 11

Elder Jacob Dyck preached in Chortitza. J. Regier preached the sermon of Thanksgiving in Neuendorf. J. Penner preached in Osterwick.

Mrs. Friesen and V. B., who had been excommunicated for adultery, were readmitted by elder Jacob Dyck. O Jesus, grant these people true repentance for their sins.

June 15

I preached the funeral sermon on Psalm 90:5,6 for the departed sister Maria Waerner of Chortitza. She passed away on June 13, 8 AM following a four-day illness. She reached the age of sixty-four years, twenty-nine weeks and a day. Her first marriage lasted fifteen years and three days. She gave birth to seven children, three of whom died. Her second marriage lasted twenty-six years and eight days. She gave birth to two children, one of whom is alive. She had thirty-five grandchildren, thirteen of whom died. “Blessed are the dead who die in the Lord.” [Rev. 14:13]

June 16

This morning elder Jacob Dyck and J. Hildebrand began their journey to Odessa on community/congregational business. The [district] secretary Gerhard Penner went as translator and the Rosenthal school teacher Johann Wieler as the coach driver. The dear Saviour go with you.

June 17
The H. Thiessens and their two children paid us a visit.

June 18
I preached in Chortitza on Psalm 39:6. Brother Peter Dyck preached in Neuendorf. Teach us to remember that we must die so that we may become wise.

June 20
My brother-in-law H. Thiessen and his family left on their return journey. The angel of the Lord accompany you.

June 22
I preached the funeral sermon for little Elisabeth Hildebrand in the Hildebrand home in Rosenthal. She died after an illness of six days on June 20, 8 PM. She was two years, one month and twenty-six days old. Jesus accepts the children.

June 25
I preached in Chortitza on Matthew 11:28. H. Penner preached in Neuendorf, P. Dyck in Osterwick. Jesus accepts those sinners who truly feel they are sinners.

June 29
Thursday. On June 19 the carpenter Peter Neufeld, who was drunk, came to me and complained that he came into the pub in Einlage when Johann Fast ordered his Russian carpenter to beat him, which he did. Today he told me that when he returned home that evening he went to Abraham Dyck, where Fast also appeared. When Fast asked him whether he had lodged a complaint against him he said yes, whereupon Fast beat him again. It turned out that Fast was not at fault in the first instance, but that the second incident was true. They forgave one another and reconciled. It was clear that Fast overreacted to Neufeld's verbal abuse. O God, when will things improve?

June 30
Jacob, Johann and I journeyed to the annual fair in Yekaterinoslav and returned on July 3. Thanks be to the Lord for his protection.

July 1

H. Penner preached in Chortitza, Johann Penner in Neuendorf. May Your blessing rest upon these sermons.

Elder Jacob Dyck and Jacob Hildebrand returned from their journey to Odessa on June 30. General Insov's stroke impaired him severely. His mouth is badly distorted and his speech barely discernible. The Lord protected their coming and going. Thanks be to Him.

July 9

I preached in Osterwick on 1 John 4:19. H. Penner preached in Chortitza, elder Jacob Dyck in Neuendorf. May we all be permeated by Your love, O Lord Jesus.

July 16

I preached in Neuendorf on Psalm 39:6. Elder Jacob Dyck preached in Chortitza. In You, O Lord, I place my complete trust. I know you will be my helper and consider my need.

Why the trip to Odessa? It came too late. It will be difficult to reclaim what was lost. The four thousand dessiatines next to Memrik settlement is no longer available to us. It is uncertain whether a second land area will become available. When elder Jacob Dyck questioned the official about the petition of the Molotschna elders regarding the reaffirmation of the *Privilegium,* he answered with a sarcastic chuckle — "It will make no difference."

On July 10 the district office received permission to order one thousand five hundred hymnbooks from Prussia. Since not all types of hymnbooks can be imported, the Guardian Committee demanded a list of all the books we wish to import.[4]

July 23

Johann Penner preached in Chortitza. H. Penner preached in Neuendorf, J. Regier in Osterwick.

On July 15 I preached a funeral sermon in Nieder-Chortitza for brother H. Penner. He died on Saturday, 2 AM after suffering dropsy for three quarters of a year. He reached the age of forty-two years, forty weeks and twenty-five days. He was married for approximately twenty years, produced four children, of whom three are alive. The Lord will be gracious to his soul and reward him with joy after his long suffering.

This afternoon my wife's cousin Abraham Doerksen and his family arrived in Chortitza from Ellenwald in Prussia. They stayed with Peter Braun because they did not know they had friends and relatives here.

July 24

A. Doerksens visited us. I held the funeral service for the departed sister Catarina Neudorf at the Schoenhorst residence of H. Penner. She died on July 22, 8:30 PM after a year-long illness which kept her bedridden. She reached the age of eighty years, nine months and two days. Her first marriage lasted thirty-eight years. She bore twelve children, five of whom died. She had forty-four grandchildren, of whom sixteen died. She had eleven great-grandchildren. Her second marriage lasted seven years. There were no children. Blessed are the dead who died in the Lord.

July 25

The Abraham Doerksens were at our house for breakfast. In the evening they began their return journey to the Molotschna. Dear ones, the Lord's angel accompany you.

I preached the funeral sermon at the Schoenberg residence of David Doerksen for the young man David Doerksen. He was ill for a long time and died on July 23 at 11 AM at the age of twenty years, three months and five days. Rest in peace.

July 30

J. Penner preached in Chortitza on Matthew 6:33. Seek you first the kingdom of God.

August 6

Elder Jacob Warkentin from Altonau preached in Chortitza.

August 9

My dear wife and I and son Diedrich travelled to Peter Siemens on the Obitisch estate and arrived there at 8 PM. Our son Diedrich and their daughter Catarina were engaged.

August 11
We and the engaged couple arrived home safe and sound at 5 PM.

August 13
P. Dyck preached in Chortitza, J. Regier in Neuendorf. The Lord bless these sermons. Yesterday evening Abraham Goerz and Jacob Kopp returned from Prussia with nine hundred hymnbooks for the Chortitza congregation.

August 16
Our children, Lenchen and Heinrich as well as Diedrich and his fiancee left for Ekaterinoslav to visit their uncle and aunt, the H. Thiessens. The Lord's angel accompany you.

August 17
On Thursday H. Hildebrand and Abraham Froese from Einlage appeared before the *Lehrdienst*. Abraham Hiebert of Chortitza got involved in a brawl in Einlage. He had got drunk at home, etc. The matter was referred to the *Bruederschaft*. Peter Thiessen of Schoenhorst quarrels with his wife, verbally abuses her, drinks excessively, etc. She does not wish to live with him. He is admonished to try to win back his wife. These are all the fruits of sin.

August 18
Our children returned from Ekaterinoslav safe and sound. Thank You for Your gracious protection.

August 20
J. Regier preached in Chortitza, Peter Dyck in Neuendorf and Johann Penner in Osterwick.

August 22
This morning our children Diedrich and his fiancee, Heinrich, Johann and Annchen drove to Peter Siemens's farm [*Chutor*] on the lands of Mr. Delbitsch. The wedding will be held on August 24. May your angel, O Lord, bring them safely there and back.

August 24

Today I presided at the wedding of Klaas Peters and Catarina Braun at the Osterwick residence of Cornelius Peters. Today brother J. Regier presided at the wedding of my children at the Peter Siemens' farm. The Lord Jesus guide their pilgrimage to His honour and the salvation of their souls.

August 26

Today David Penner, Claas Dyck, Regier, Jacob Klassen came to get our David Penner for work in the Molotschna. They left for the community sheep farm [where David Penner worked].

August 27

Jacob Regier preached in Chortitza, P. Dyck in Neuendorf.

August 28

I travelled to the community farm. The family of David Penner left for the Molotschna on August 29. He will remain there until the cattle-pest has run its course. When they left it seemed Mrs. Penner was angry and irate for no apparent reason. May the Saviour forgive her this sin. Dear ones—may the Lord's angel go with you.

September 2

A number of immigrants (our co-religionists) arrived here in Chortitza. Among them was a young man Jacob Epp, a son of my cousin Jacob Epp. After a two-hour stopover they left for the Molotschna.

September 3

Elder Jacob Dyck preached in Chortitza. Jacob Regier preached in Neuendorf, Peter Dyck in Osterwick. God is love.

Bruederschaft. Abraham Hiebert of Chortitza apologized to the congregation and was forgiven. These things are done so casually (pro forma).

September 6

I took our children the David Epps to the community farm, where he is to become the administrator. The Lord give him wisdom in running the farm. Be with them, O dear Saviour.

September 7
I returned safely this evening. Praise and thanks to you, O Saviour.

September 8
The Niemans from Muensterberg arrived for a visit this morning.

September 9
This morning we travelled to Yekaterinoslav. In the evening the H. Friesens from Blumenort and their three children arrived at my brother-in-law's. The H. Thiessens arrived at the J. Dycks.

September 10
This morning both the Friesens and sister H. Thiessen paid us a visit.

Elder Jacob Dyck preached in Chortitza on Matthew 7: 13-14. Peter Dyck preached in Neuendorf. Give [us] strength, O Holy Jesus, to strive to enter the narrow gate.

In the afternoon I presided at the marriage of H. Sawatzky and Catarina Braun at the Kronstal residence of Peter Dyck. Enrich this marriage with your blessing, Holy Jesus.

September 11
The H. Friesens and our son Heinrich left to visit our children on the community farm.

September 12
The Niemans returned from Yekaterinoslav this evening. In the afternoon elder Jacob Dyck and Jacob Regier left for Bergthal to celebrate holy communion and preside over a ministerial election.

September 15
The Niemans left in the morning, the H. Friesens in the afternoon. The latter took our common grandchild, little H. Friesen, with them in order to further his upbringing. The Lord's angel accompany them.

September 16
Our children David, Jacob, and Johann drove to the community farm. On their return journey they brought Mrs. Friesen with them.

September 17

I preached in Chortitza on Hebrews 2:1-3, Johann Penner preached in Osterwick. May we all remain on the true pathway.

In the afternoon I preached the funeral sermon on Hebrews 13:14 for the departed sister Elisabeth Braun in the Rosenthal home of Wilhelm Siemens. She died of a stroke during the morning of September 14. She was unable to speak for three days and three nights. She reached the age of fifty-seven years, four weeks and four days. She had two children with her first husband, both of whom are still alive. Her second marriage lasted thirteen years. She had five children, four of whom are still alive. Her third marriage lasted twenty and one-half years, but there were no children. She had eighteen grandchildren, sixteen of whom are still alive. A single stroke can change everything and bring death. Be merciful to us, O Lord.

September 19

I presided at the marriage of Jacob Wiebe and Anna Dyck at the Chortitza residence of Peter Dyck. The Lord bless the union.

I preached the funeral sermon for the son of Aron Peters of Einlage. He died on September 17 at 5 PM after a three-week illness. He reached the age of eleven years, six months and four days. Rest in peace, young plant, as you wait to awaken in the eternal spring.

September 20

Elder Jacob Dyck, H. Penner and J. Regier returned from Bergthal, where they celebrated holy communion. Abraham Klassen and Jacob Wiebe were elected as ministers, Peter Epp as deacon by majority vote. Give true wisdom and anointing, Lord Jesus, for the exercise of these offices.

September 21

I preached in Chortitza on Matt. 5:6. H. Penner preached in Neuendorf. O Saviour Lord Jesus, grant us a genuine hunger and thirst for your righteousness.

September 27

This afternoon we received word that Mrs. Peter Siemens near Dalbitsch was very ill and desired to see her children. Next day I sent

Jacob to our children the Epps on the community farm. That afternoon I received word that Mrs. Siemens had died. Our children arrived in the evening and left next morning for Dalbitsch.

September 28

Thursday. Johann Sawatzky, now engaged, appeared before the *Lehrdienst* in the Chortitza church. The daughter of Wilhelm Friesen in Bergthal claimed he had an affair with her. He denied it. Similarly a Wiens from [Bergthal] claimed he had slept with the now Mrs. Gerhard Sawatsky before she was married. She admitted that he had pressured her, but asserted that she had steadily refused him. She declared her innocence amid tears. Gerhard Braun, the son-in-law of J. von Kampen was accused of theft. All these matters were referred to a [later] Sunday *Bruederschaft*. O Lord, have mercy on us.

September 30

The body [of Mrs. Peter Siemens] arrived at Siemens in Chortitza at 10 AM. That afternoon I preached her funeral sermon on ? She died on Thursday, 1 AM after an illness of nine days. She reached the age of forty-three years, six months and days. She was married for twenty-four years, four months and twenty days. She had six children, all of whom are alive. The Lord grant her a gentle and blessed rest and a blessed resurrection on that day.

October 1

I preached the harvest and Thanksgiving sermon in Neuendorf. Elder Jacob Dyck preached in Chortitza, H. Penner in Osterwick. Lord Jesus, in your grace grant us a blessed harvest in eternity.

Bruederschaft. Gerhard Braun was excommunicated from the congregation.

October 8

Brother H. Penner preached in Chortitza. J. Penner preached in Nieder-Chortitza, Peter Dyck in Neuendorf.

Bruederschaft. Braun and Sawatzky were readmitted as members in the congregation by elder Jacob Dyck. Since we are not experiencing the power of the Word, we follow the letter of the law.

Mr. and Mrs. Aron Esau from Halbstadt dropped by for a three hour visit in the evening.

October 15

Brother Johann Penner preached in Chortitza. H. Penner preached in Neuendorf, Jacob Regier in Osterwick. May the Lord bless these sermons.

At 11:15 AM my dear wife safely delivered a healthy daughter Catarina. Thank you, O Lord Jesus, for all you have done and are doing for us.

October 17

I presided at the marriage of Gerhard Penner and Anganeta Dyck at the home of Martin Dyck in Einlage. Accompany this marriage with your blessing, Jesus.

October 19

I presided at the wedding of Johann Sawatzky and Anganeta Toews at the home of Peter Loewen in Chortitza. The Lord bless this marriage.

Thursday. David Karolus and his wife from Schoenberg, Abraham Hiebert and his wife from Nieder Chortitza and the wife of Michael Loetzky appeared before the *Lehrdienst*. According to Mrs. Hiebert, her husband had spent time with Mrs. Karolus and Mrs. Loetzky, and danced and drank with them. Due to illness Hiebert did not appear. The matter will be further investigated. The others were reconciled.

October 22

Johann Peter preached in Chortitza on John 3:25, 26. Peter Dyck preached in Neuendorf, Jacob Regier in Blumengart. "Wake up O sleeper..." [Eph. 5:14].

October 24

I preached the funeral sermon in Neuendorf on ? for our departed member Gerhard Martens. He died on October 21, 5 AM following an illness of fourteen days. He reached the age of thirty-three years, three weeks and two days. He was married for eight years and four months and sired two children, one of whom died. His liquor consumption shortened his days. When will the community take action? How do we overcome this evil?

October 28

I preached the funeral sermon on ? for the tenant [Anwohner] Cornelius Vogt of Einlage. He died in the pub on the morning of October 26. He was a heavy drinker. He was fifty-eight years old. His first marriage lasted three years and he sired one daughter who is still alive. His second marriage lasted twenty-four years. He sired three children, one of whom died. His third marriage lasted three and one-half years and produced two children, both of whom are alive. He had eleven grandchildren, three of whom died. His spiritual life was pathetic. Twice God saved him from the jaws of death. Each time he joked about it and continued to drink. Saviour be merciful to him.

October 29

I preached in Chortitza on Ephesians 3:18, 19. Johann Penner preached in Neuendorf, Heinrich Penner in Osterwick. Love is better than all wisdom.

November 5

Elder Jacob Dyck preached in Chortitza, Jacob Regier in Neuendorf. Bless this see, O Lord, for Your glory and to the salvation of our souls.

November 12

Jacob Regier preached in Chortitza, P. D. in Neuendorf, H. Penner in Einlage. Bless this for your glory.

November 19

I preached in Burwalde? on Matt. 6:9-13. J. Regier preached in Chortitza, H. Penner in Neuendorf, ? in Osterwick. "Ask and it will be given to you; seek and you will find; knock and the door will be opened to you." [Matt. 7:7]

Bruederschaft. Mrs. Karolus and Jacob Giesbrecht had an affair and were excommunicated from the congregation. May the dear Saviour grant them true repentance.

November 21

I presided at the marriage of Wilhelm Reinke and Helena Martens at the Einlage residence of Peter Jansz. The Lord bless them.

November 26

A general *Bruederschaft* to elect deacons and ministers. Three deacons were elected. David Wiensz from Kronstal with one hundred and thirty-nine votes; Heinrich Penner from Schoenhorst with eighty-eight votes; Dirk Dyck from Chortitza with forty-four votes. One hundred and seventy-eight brethren cast their votes. Two ministers were elected from the deacons: Jacob Dyck from Chortitza with one hundred and thirty-nine votes; David Wiensz from Kronstal with one hundred and fifty votes. One hundred and seventy-four brethren cast their votes. Endow these men with wisdom and power for their office, O Lord Jesus. Amen.[5]

David Wiensz, Jacob Dyck and Dirk Dyck, who were present, accepted their offices. Heinrich Penner from Schoenhorst who was not present, will give his answer to the *Lehrdienst* this coming Sunday.

Following the elections Jacob Giesbrecht and Mrs. Karolus from Nieder Chortitza were readmitted to the congregation by elder Jacob Dyck. Dear Jesus, accept the repentance for this sin.

December 3

Elder Jacob Dyck preached in Chortitza on Luke 21: 25-36. Jacob Regier preached in Neuendorf, Peter Dyck in Osterwick, Johann Penner in Blumengart. Make us attentive to Your Word, O Lord. The elected deacon H. Penner from Schoenhorst appeared before the *Lehrdienst* and accepted his office. Lord grant him strength to fulfil his calling.

December 6

I preached the funeral sermon on ? for Maria Hausknecht at the Hausknecht home in Einlage. She died on December 4, 5 AM following a three-week illness at the age of twenty-nine weeks. Jesus said: "Let the little children come to me, and do not hinder them…" [Mark 10:14].

December 9

I preached the funeral sermon on ? for the departed brother Abraham Krahn in the home of Peter Krahn. He was ill for a long time but did not want to accept his death. Eight days before he died the

Lord led him past the portals of death. Finally he relented. There is joy with the angels when such a one repents. He died on December 5 at 6 AM at the age of twenty-five years, eight weeks and one day. He was married for one year and thirteen days. There were no children. The Lord is near to those who call upon Him.

December 10

H. Penner preached in Chortitza, Peter Dyck in Osterwick, J. Regier in Neuendorf. Prepare us all to appear before you Lord Jesus.

December 17

I preached in Neuendorf on ? H. Penner preached in Chortitza, ? in Osterwick. Be with us all Lord Jesus.

December 24

I preached in Chortitza on Zechariah 9:9. H. Penner preached in Neuendorf. May we give you a worthy reception Lord Jesus.

December 25

I preached in Osterwick on John 1:14. Elder Jacob Dyck preached in Chortitza on Luke 2: 8-14, H. Penner preached in Neuendorf, Johann Penner in ? Come into all of our hearts Lord Jesus.

December 26

I preached in Chortitza on Isaiah 9:6. Elder Jacob Dyck preached in Osterwick. Peter Dyck preached in Neuendorf, Jacob Regier in Nieder-Chortitza, Johann Penner in Blumengart. Praise and thanks to you, Lord Jesus, for the love you have shown us.

December 27

I and our son travelled to Yekaterinoslav on business.

December 31

We arrived home at noon. Thanks to the Lord Jesus for His gracious leading.

The last Sunday [of the year]. Johann Penner preached in Chortitza, Peter Dyck in Neuendorf, H. Penner in Osterwick. In the afternoon I preached the funeral sermon for Jacob, the infant son of Abraham Jansz the watchmaker, at the residence of Johann Gerbrand. He died on December 26 following an illness of two days. He was four weeks, three days old. "Let the little children come to me, and do not hinder them." [Mark 10:14]

In the past year three hundred and thirteen children were born, one hundred and forty-three males, one hundred and seventy females. Eighty-three men and seventy-nine women died, one hundred and fifty-two in all. The overall increase was one hundred and sixty-one. There were forty-nine marriages.

Spring and summer proved productive. The late summer was very hot with dust storms. The hay crop was very good. Winter rye was poor while the spring crops were average. Fall saw a good deal of rain. Winter began on St. Martin's day with much snow and drifting and temperatures to minus 21°. The winter rye had germinated.

Around Christmas time the price of hay ranged from two hundred and twenty to two hundred and forty rubles per load. The price of rye increased from six rubles to thirteen and fourteen rubles per *chetvert*. Wheat was fifteen rubles [per *chetvert*]. Oats sold between two and eight rubles, barley from two and one half to ten rubles, millet five to eight rubles [per *chetvert*], butter from thirty-five to eighty kopecks per pound.

Congregational life leaves much to be desired. We move along according to convention, but without true spiritual life. Watchman, is the night soon past? In the Molotschna the torch of discord burns brightly. Where is the water to quench it—on the blood-stained hill of Golgotha!

We have experienced frequent cloudbursts with hail the size of chicken eggs. Everywhere there are storms, hurricanes, earthquakes, great fires and great floods. Terrible storms and an almost unbearable heat during July and August—these are all warning signs inviting humanity to repent.

Because peace reigns and no one senses the danger, we continue to live as in the time of Noah.... The [end] time is near. Go forth and preach the Gospel to all peoples—this is happening through missions and Bible distribution. There are faithful witnesses on Mt. Zion proclaiming the great message that only in Jesus is there forgiveness for our sins. He will save those from destruction who desire to be saved. Hallelujah! Amen.[6]

Endnotes

[1] David Epp's networking provides some interesting perspectives. While in Ohrloff he visits Heinrich Heese the teacher in the *Vereinsschule* (Society School) and spends some time with the estate owner Johann Cornies. Perhaps this still reflected something of the sense of egalitarianism characterizing the Mennonite society of that day, which allowed a poor man like Epp to informally visit with the wealthiest Mennonite in New Russia. Similarly his interaction with Peter Schmidt of Steinbach, the teachers Lange and Friesen as well as district mayor Toews reflect a certain freedom of interaction amidst Russian Mennonites.

[2] The concern with the *Privilegium* was a long-standing issue. Living under tzarist autocracy essentially meant seeking a reaffirmation of the document at the commencement of each successive reign. Why such a petition was thought necessary in the middle of Nicholas's reign (1825-1855) is unclear, unless it was simply to alert the tzar to one of many minorities in his vast empire. Elder Jacob Dyck's objection to the action (February 20) was, in Epp's estimation, based on jealousy.

[3] Depression or mental illness was frequently diagnosed as a spiritual issue.

[4] The decision to import 1,500 hymnals from Prussia tells us something about the status of print culture among the Russian Mennonites. In all likelihood the hymnal in question relates to the *Geistreiches Gesangbuch*, first published in 1767, which went through ten editions until it was replaced in 1869. The Chortitza church probably purchased the eighth edition of the hymnal, published in Marienburg in 1838. Russian Mennonites later published their own editions of the Prussian Mennonite hymnal, beginning in Odessa in 1844.

[5] It is not clear from Epp's diary entry whether there were candidates other than the ones elected. Perhaps the voters could cast three ballots each for the deacons, two for the ministers. Generally the call of the congregation was looked upon as the call of God and the candidate, however inexperienced, usually accepted.

[6] David Epp's pessimism with regard to the spiritual state of the settlement permeates his entire diary. His participation in the *Lehrdienst* and *Bruederschaft* meant a knowledge of every known sin in the community and no doubt contributed to his gloomy outlook. Personally he was a person of exacting morality and deep piety. He naturally found it difficult to understand people who did not share his level of commitment. Then too, visiting missionaries and Bible Society representatives provided him with a glimpse of a more vital Christianity than he observed in the day-to-day life of the settlement.

The Mennonite church in Chortitza

1840

January 1

"For me to live is Christ and to die is gain." [Phil. 1:21] "Praise the Lord, O my soul. All my inmost being praise his holy name." [Psalm 103:1] "He forgives all my sins and heals all my diseases; he redeems my life from the pit and crowns me with love and compassion" [Psalm 103:3-4]. Praise the Lord, O my soul, and experience His measureless grace.

New Year's day. I preached in Neuendorf on Ephesians 4:22-24. Elder Jacob Dyck preached in Chortitza on the same text. H. Penner preached in Osterwick, Jacob Regier in Einlage. Grant us, Lord Jesus, new strength for a God-pleasing walk in this new year.

January 2

I preached the funeral sermon on Hebrews 13:14 in the Osterwick school for little Jacob, the son of the school teacher Jacob Dyck. He passed away on January 1 at 10 AM at the age of one year, two months and ten days following a ten-day illness. "Blessed are the dead who die in the Lord" [Rev. 14:13].

Thursday *Lehrdienst*. A complaint was filed by Isaac Kasdorf of the Schoenwiese congregation against David Braun of Einlage concerning the sale of sheep. The complaint was accepted by elder Jacob Dyck without informing elder Jacob Hildebrand. The parties were reconciled.

The young man Jacob Neufeld was engaged to the daughter of D. Epp from Nieder Chortitza. The engagement was announced to the congregation on two occasions. Now they had mutually agreed to separate. They were reminded that they had pledged themselves to one another at the formal engagement celebration. The bridegroom and the stepfather of the bride will explain the reasons for the separation to the congregation this coming Sunday. This is the first time during my thirty-three years of public service that this has happened. Are we making new rules? Will this attitude spread?[1]

January 6
I preached in Chortitza on Matthew 2:1-10. Jacob Dyck preached in Neuendorf, Jacob Regier in Osterwick, elder Jacob Dyck in Neuenberg. Lead us, Lord Jesus, that we might stay on the correct pathway.

January 7
On this first Sunday of the year, I preached in Neuendorf on Acts 27:25. David Wiensz preached in Chortitza on Psalm 32:8. It was his first sermon. Instruct us in your paths Lord. Amen.

January 9
I presided over the marriage of Peter Siemens and Margareta Breul at the Peter Breul residence in Rosenthal. May it be a good marriage.

January 10
Thursday. Gerhard Siemens from Chortitza appeared before the *Lehrdienst* on charges of drinking strong liquor. He admitted it. He was admonished, promised to reform and was dismissed.

The *Comitaet* [Odessa] did not accept the hymnbooks sent by elder Dyck and has sent them back. This issue may yet come back to haunt us. Perhaps this experience will teach us something.[2]

I reported that Jacob Krahn, son of Jacob Krahn and his bride separated after two public announcements of their engagement. Elder Jacob Dyck did not seem too concerned.

It has been rumoured that the newly elected deacon Dirk Dyck sold flour mixed with sand in Yekaterinoslav. His companion had split stolen wood in a cellar. Dirk Dyck said he knew of nothing of all this.

He had been told to deliver some split [fire]wood and did so. He did nothing else. "If any of you is without sin, let him be the first to throw a stone" [John 8:7].

January 14

Jacob Dyck preached in Chortitza on Mark 1:16. It was his first sermon. Peter Dyck preached in Neuendorf, David Wiensz in Osterwick on Psalm 32:8.

January 18

I presided at the wedding of Dirk Neufeld and Anna Ens at the Isaac Ens residence in Nieder Chortitza. Bless this marriage Lord Jesus.

Thursday. The following appeared before the *Lehrdienst*: the carpenter Peter Neufeld from Einlage; Jacob Andreas Junior; the sons of Gerhard Rempel, Gerd and Dirk; Heinrich ? Isaac and his bride; Jacob Isaac; Dirk Toews from Rosengart. Neufeld and the Rempel boys had been drinking. Bridegroom [Isaac] decided to walk to [Jacob] Andreas, but Neufeld and the two Rempel brothers refused to let his bride go with him. Then around 10 PM the Rempel brothers walked over to the [Jacob] Andreas and asked him to go to Neufeld and bring back [Isaac's] bride. When Andreas arrived Neufeld attacked him, but Andreas valiantly defended himself. The Rempel brothers pulled them apart and Andreas went home without his cap. In the morning Andreas went to retrieve his cap but found the door locked. He forced one of the doors and walked in. He asked for his cap but received no answer from the [drunken?] figure lying in the bed. Since Neufeld owed him money for liquor he took Neufeld's coat as security and left. The young couple reconciled [over the incident]. Dirk Toews and Isaac also reconciled with the others, all of whom were at odds with one another. The others [who refused to reconcile?] will be dealt with by the brethren [*Bruederschaft*]. It seems we have earned such situations by our sins of omission.

January 21

David Wiens preached in Chortitza on ? Jacob Dyck preached in Neuendorf on Mark 1:16....

Bruederschaft. Johann Andreas was the first to appear before the congregation. He acknowledged his shortcoming, apologized and received forgiveness. Peter Neufeld insisted he was in the right and was excommunicated by the congregation. The Rempels promised to reform and the congregation, hopeful of this, forgave them in this instance. "Your word is a lamp to my feet and a light for my path." [Psalm 119:105]

January 25

Thursday. Joseph Kornelsen appeared before the *Lehrdienst* and accused Johann Harder of Rosenthal of stealing a goose from him and that Mrs. Harder killed a goose belonging to him. Harder replied that a goose had lain on his table, but he insisted that he killed only one goose. Afterall Kornelsen's geese were damaging his grain pile. His [Harder's] wife had not killed a goose. Harder insisted he had not stolen anything and Kornelsen could offer no proof. [The *Lehrdienst*] urged reconciliation, but it did not take place. Kornelsen intimated that elder Jacob Dyck did not take the theft seriously. He was told this was an insult [to elder Dyck].... God only knows where all this will lead.

January 26

Bruederschaft. Kornelsen and Harder have been reconciled. Kornelsen apologized for insulting elder Jacob Dyck. He did so in the ministerial meeting room [*Ohmsstube*].

1. Elder Jacob Dyck presented another case to the brethren. Some time ago the elected deacon Dirk Dyck from Chortitza sold flour mixed with sand in Ekaternoslav. He also split and used stolen wood. An unsigned letter has been found which made similar charges. Dirk Dyck was asked to leave the room. For a time there was only a murmuring among the brethren. Finally the school teacher Klippenstein from Schoenhorst said that he had heard that Dyck had used stolen wood. He was asked who gave him this information. He replied that it was F. Wall from Blumengart. Wall was not present. Klippenstein was asked to appear before the *Kirchenkonvent* this coming Thursday. Two brethren were assigned to make sure Wall was present. Elias Baergen from Schoenhorst asserted that Dyck had sold eggs filled with sand. When asked how he knew this he replied that Dietrich Thiessen had told him and that Cornelius Thiessen from the *chutor* had also been present. The meeting was informed that Cornelius Thiessen belonged to the Kronsweide congregation. [Someone] remarked that eggs filled with

sand were easily distinguishable from others because of their weight

The entire issue seemed rather silly [to me] and so I said that the matter was a bit like wanting to hang someone because he had sold fine potatoes in place of salt. Cornelius Kopp stood up and wondered whether Dirk Dyck had filled the eggs with sand as an act of mischief against Johann Penner. In response Wilhelm Thiessen from Rosengart asserted that, based on his contacts with him, Dyck was a reliable person.

Dyck [was called back into the room] and was asked to respond to the charges. He spoke freely and, claiming God was his witness, declared his innocence.

Pauls from Neuendorf asserted that a businessman in Ekaterinoslav said he [Dyck] should have been whipped because he mixed sand with flour. I interrupted Pauls and asked him . . . if the person had [specifically] identified Dyck. "No, he only said it was a German," Pauls replied. I asked Dyck about filling egg shells with sand and selling them. He replied that a market woman in Ekaterinoslav had returned an egg filled with sand to him, and that he felt embarrassed.

"Who sent the egg [with you]?"

"The people from Blumengart who gave it to me should know that."

Cornielius Kopp again stood up and spoke to the issue. Dyck was asked to return to his seat, which he did. Satan was a liar from the beginning and people are deceived and believe his lies. He has his "work in those who are disobedient"[Eph. 2:2].[3]

2. Elder Jacob Dyck asked the brethren for their indulgence since the hymnbooks had to be sent to the *Comitaet* in Odessa.

3.The community was encouraged to continue with the tree planting.

4. Preparations for holy communion would begin this coming Sunday in Chortitza and Neuendorf. The brethren were encouraged to [reconcile and] unify. They were to come to the Lord's Table as repentant sinners.

The *Bruederschaft* ended peaceably.

January 28

Elder Jacob Dyck preached the preparatory sermon in Chortitza. H. Penner preached in Neuendorf; J. preached in Osterwick on Luke

14:13. Jesus accepts us sinners.

February 1

Thursday. Klippenstein from Schoenhorst and Froese from Blumengart appeared before the *Kirchenkonvent* regarding the Dirk Dyck affair [see January 26]. Froese admitted speaking to Klippenstein [about Dyck] when he in fact knew nothing [concerning the case]. Elder Jacob Dyck suggested Dirk Dyck should withdraw [from the deaconate?] That was wrong [of him]. "You shall not give false testimony against your neighbour." [Ex. 20:16]

February 4

Elder Jacob Dyck celebrated holy communion with one hundred and seventy members in the Chortitza church. I was at our community sheep farm and did not attend. Peter Dyck preached in Neuendorf. Jesus accepts sinners. Amen.

February 8

I preached the funeral sermon on Psalm 39:5-6 for our departed member, Maria Penner, in the home of the tenant [*Anwohner*], Peter Penner. She died on Sunday, 5 PM, after a severe illness of four days. She reached the age of forty-three years, two months. She was married for eighteen years and seventeen days and gave birth to three sons and five daughters all of whom are alive. "Teach us to number our days aright, that we may gain a heart of wisdom" [Psa. 90:12].

February 11

Elder Jacob Dyck celebrated holy communion with two hundred and twenty-two members of the Neuendorf congregation. I came as a poor guest to Your table. Jacob Penner preached the thanksgiving sermon in Chortitza. The goodness of the Lord is so great.

February 18

I preached in Neuendorf on Ephesians 1:3. H. Penner preached the thanksgiving sermon in Osterwick. Jacob Dyck preached in Chortitza, Jacob Penner in Rosengart. Thank you Lord for all the benefits you bestow on us.

On February 17 at 10 PM our daughter Mrs. B. Friesen gave birth to a healthy son. His name is David. May he grow up to the Lord's glory.

February 24

This morning at 2:30 AM the farm building of Jacob Dyck of Rosenthal went up in flames. His wife and daughter died in the inferno. Their bodies were pulled out of the ashes with hands and feet missing. The survivors escaped in their night shirts barefooted. All the sheep died in the fire as well as almost all the cattle and horses. All his implements except two wagons, a sleigh and a plough standing on the yard were destoryed. His home and handiwork are all in ashes. He survived with burns on his hands and face and other wounds—but without his wife and daughter. "How unsearchable his judgements and his paths beyond tracing out." [Rom. 11:33][4]

February 25

I preached in Chortitza on Isaiah 53:4. David Wiens preached in Neuendorf, Jacob Regier in Nieder Chortitza. "Can a mother forget the baby at her breast? . . . Though she may forget, I will not forget you!" [Isa. 49:15-16]

February 27

I preached the funeral sermon on Isaiah 48:10 for our member, sister Maria Dyck, and her seven-year-old daugher Anna who both perished in the fire. She reached the age of twenty-eight years, one month and twenty-four days. She was married for eight years and one month. She bore three sons and two daughters, of whom two sons and one daughter died. God will reward [Maria's] motherly love.

March 3

I preached in Chortitza on Isaiah 53:7. Jacob Regier preached in Neuendorf, H. Penner in Osterwick "The Lord is near to all who call on him." [Psalm 145:18]

March 4

This morning Reverend Peter Dyck died of a throat infection after a brief illness. May the loving Saviour grant him eternal joy.

March 6

He [Peter Dyck] was buried. Elder Jacob Dyck preachd the funeral sermon. May the Lord grant him his portion. Daniel 12:3. Our neighbour Peter Ensz was [also] buried. Heinrich Penner preached the funeral sermon. He was ill for twenty-two weeks and died of congestive heart failure. "He will wipe every tear from their eyes" [Rev. 21:4].

March 7

I presided over the wedding of Bernd Rempel, my sister's son, and Margareta Bergmann at the home of my brother-in-law Dirk Rempel of Schoenhorst. May the Lord grant them a happy marriage.

Thursday. Jacob Unrau from Kronsweide, Jacob Penner from Einlage and Gerhard Rempel, son of G.R., appeared before the *Kirchenkonvent*. Penner had been drinking. He was given a warning and promised to better himself. He was forgiven. The other three had made and consumed several flasks of wine. They tried to excuse themselves but finally admitted their fault and asked for forgiveness. The matter was deferred for decision by the brethern on Sunday. Each person must give an account of himself.

March 10

I preached in Neuendorf on Luke 22:39-44. Elder Jacob Dyck preached in Chortitza. "Your rod and your staff they comfort me" [Psa. 23:4].

Bruederschaft. Unrau, Braun and Rempel were excommuinicated from the congregation. May the Lord grant them the true spirit of repentance.

March 17

Elder Jacob Dyck preached in Chortitza. H. Penner preached in Neuendorf. D. Wiensz in Osterwick. May I always think of your suffering and pain.

Bruederschaft. Cornelius Martens of Einlage had purchased a home and *Anwohner* [tenant] lot from Peter Neufeld, who did not to belong to the congregation. He asked the brethren to forgive them and they did so. A long neglected regulation appears to have re-emerged.[5]

March 24

H. Penner preached in Chortitza on Isaiah 43:24, 25. Elder Jacob Dyck preached in Neuendorf. Heal me, O my Savior, for I am very ill.

March 31

H. Penner preached in Chortitza on Matthew 26:36-3?. Johann Penner preached in Neuendorf, David Wiens in Osterwick. Lord Jesus, bless these messages.

Bruederschaft. Dirk Braun and Rempel from Einlage were readmitted as members of the congregation by elder Jacob Dyck. Purge their sins, dear Lord, according to your great mercy.

April 3

I preached the funeral sermon for our departed member and brother Martin Tilitsky at the home of Peter Braun in Neuendorf. He was ill for eleven weeks and died on March 31 at 6:30 AM at the age of sixty-seven years. His first marriage lasted some seventeen and one-half years, his second nine years and three weeks. He had no children from his second marriage. His remains will rest in the grave. I wish him a joyous resurrection and the inheritance of the children of God.

April 7

Palm Sunday. I preached in Osterwick on Matthew 21:1-19. J. Regier preached in Chortitza, H. Penner in Neuendorf. My Lord, allow us to bring to You our weaknesses and shortcomings.

April 12

Good Friday. I preached in Neuendorf on John 19:28-30. Elder Jacob Dyck preached in Chortitza on 2 Corinthians 5:21, J. Regier preached in Osterwick. Our Saviour, who died for our sins, give me strength to die to sin and to live for you.

April 14

The first day of Easter. I preached in Rosengart on Mark 16:1-8. Elder Jacob Dyck preached in Chortitza, H. Penner in Neuendorf, D. Wiensz in Osterwick, Jakob Penner in Burwalde. I believe with all my heart that Christ rose from the dead through the power of the Father. He has taken away the power of death. Hallelujah! It was announced in all the churches that a ministerial election will be held in the church on April 16.

April 15

The second day of Easter. I preached in Chortitza on Luke 24:13-36. ? preached in Neuendorf, J. Regier in Osterwick, Johann Penner in Blumengart. "The Lord is my shepherd." [Psalm 23:1] On Good Friday Unrau from Kronsweide was again accepted as a member of the congregation by elder Jacob Dyck.

April 16

The third day of Easter. Elections were held in the Chortitza church. Two deacons were elected. Johann Dyck of Neuendorf with one hundred and thirty-five votes, Jacob Wiensz of Kronstal with fifty-nine votes. One hundred and ninety-seven brethren voted. Two ministers were elected: Heinrich Penner, the deacon from Schoenhorst was elected with one hundred and eighty votes; Wiensz from Kronsweide with one hundred and forty-six. One hundred and seventy-three brethren cast their votes. The dear Saviour grant them strength for this important service.

April 18

I preached the funeral sermon on Hebrews 13:14 in the Nieder Chortitza home of Peter Mantler for our departed member, sister Maria Mantler. She died on the second day of Easter at 8 PM after an illness of eight months. She reached the age of forty-seven years, nine months and fourteen days. She was married for twenty-nine years and gave birth to seven sons and eleven daughters, of whom two sons and two daughters died. She had five grandchildren, two of whom died. "He will wipe away every tear from their eyes" [Rev. 21:4].

April 21

Using Romans 10:10. I presented the articles of faith in Neuendorf for the first time. Elder Jacob Dyck did the same in Chortitza. "Faith without deeds is dead" [James 2:26]. The newly elected teachers and deacons, Dyck and Wiensz, sat in the places [designated for such offices].

April 25

I preached the funeral sermon for our departed member Wilhelm Zachrias in the home of the deceased. He died on April 22 at 2:30 AM following an illness of four weeks. He reached the age of seventy-one years, one month, three weeks and four days. His first marriage lasted eleven years and he sired three sons, one of whom died. His second marriage lasted thirty-eight years. He sired twelve sons and four daughters, of whom eight sons and two daughters died. He had thirty-six grandchildren, of whom sixteen died. He had one great-granchild. His loins generated fifty-six souls. "The day of death [is] better than the day of birth" [Ecc. 7:1]. The one brings us into a world of suffering, the other into a world of joy.

April 28

I presented the articles of faith to the Neuendorf congregation to the end of article eight. Elder Jacob Dyck did the same in Chortitza. Lord, awaken our faith.

May 5

I presented the rest of the articles of faith in Neuendorf for the third time. Elder Dyck did so in Chortitza. In Neuendorf thirty-two candidates of both genders applied for holy baptism, in Chortitza there were ? candidates. "But small is the gate and narrow the road that leads to life, and only a few find it" [Matt. 7:14].

May 7

I preached the funeral sermon on ? for our departed member and sister, the widow Helena Wiebe of Schoenberg, at the Abraham Reimer residence. She died of a stroke after a three-day illness on May 4, at 2 AM at the age of eighty-two. Her two marriages lasted a total of forty-five years. In her first marriage she gave birth to fourteen children, nine of whom died. She had seventy-five grandchildren and eighteen great-grandchildren. She will rest in peace until the end of time.

May 12

I presented the articles of faith (to article nine) to the Neuendorf congregation while elder Jacob Dyck did so in Neuendorf. It was the fourth presentation. There are thirty-three candidates of both genders in Neuendorf, ? in Chortitza. Without a true, heartfelt faith it is impossible to please God. Cornelius Eitzen, who was not a member of the congregation for many years, was accepted into to the church by elder Jacob Dyck. God only knows if this was a good thing....

May 13

Hildebrand a young man from Neuenburg newly married in fall, drowned while helping with the sheep dipping. The Lord will be gracious to his soul.

May 16

I and Dirk Rempel Senior travelled to visit Peter Friesen of Schoenberg who had contracted rabies from an infected dog. He had torn the clothes on his right arm and torn up his shirt. We prepared a mixture of ? and when it was ready in the evening we gave it to him to drink. He drank a lot and it was effective. Thank you God he is getting better. I told him he must keep drinking it if he wished to recover.

May 18

This evening the dear brothers Lange and Peter Schmidt arrived from Steinbach. They stayed the night. In the morning they continued their journey to Ekaterinoslav. The Lord accompany you dear ones.

On May 16 Abraham Jansz and Johann Funk from Neuendorf appeared before the *Kirchenkonvent* in Chortitza. They had gotten into a big fight and refused to be reconciled. They were admonished and subsequently settled their differences. "Forgive and you will be forgiven" [Luke 6:37].

May 19

I presented the articles of faith in Neuendorf for the fifth time. Elder Dyck did likewise in Chortitza. In Neuendorf there are fifteen male and eighteen female candidates for holy baptism; in Chortitza forty female and forty male candidates. God write their names in the book of life. Give them a place near the Lamb nailed to the cross for us.

The young lady Wilhelmina Hausknecht, the stepdaughter of C.A. Hausknecht, was registered as a baptismal candidate according to our customary pattern. She had been separated from her parents in Warsaw as a child and had been sent to our colony by chief justice Ladejav and, according to his instruction, registered here.

It was also decided to introduce a levy for the support of the poor and to cover other community expenses. Every farmstead is to pay two rubles and every member of the congregation one ruble and seventy-five kopecks. The mayors are to prepare the list of contributors, collect the money and present both the list and the money to the *Kirchenkonvent*.[6]

On May 17 at 8:30 AM our daughter-in-law, Mrs. D. Epp, successfully delivered a baby boy named David. The dear Saviour grant them happiness with this child.

May 21

Pentecost. Elder Jacob Dyck catechized eighty baptismal candidates in Chortitza. There were three candidates from Krongarten. Bless this undertaking Lord Jesus.

May 23

Ascension Day. I preached in Neuendorf on ? . Elder Dyck preached in Chortitza, ? in Osterwick. I catechized thirty-three candidates [in Neuendorf] and elder Jacob Dyck eighty [in Chortitza].

May 26

Elder Jacob Dyck presented the articles of faith to the congregation for the sixth time. The baptismal candidates, eighty in all sat on the front benches—their heads uncovered, the hair [of the young ladies] braided. I catechized the thirty-three candidates of both genders in Neuendorf. Bless the seed that has been sown, O Lord.

May 28

I and our son Jacob travelled to Yekaterinoslav on business. Similarly our children the B. Friesens and ? travelled to ? The Lord's angel go with them.

May 30

I returned from Yekaterinoslav safe and sound. Thanks be to the Saviour.

June 1

Our children the Dirk Epps arrived from the community sheep farm for a visit, as did my brother-in-law Jacob Stoess, his wife and two children.

June 2

The first day of Pentecost. Elder Jacob Dyck preached in Chortitza on John 3:16-21. H. Penner preached in Neuendorf, Johann Penner in Osterwick, Jacob Regier in [Burwalde?]. May the Holy Spirit come to us all. Amen. This evening our brother-in-law Jacob Stoess left to visit friends.

June 3

The second day of Pentecost. In Chortitza elder Jacob Dyck baptized the following candidates: seventy-seven from Chortitza; three from Kronsgarten; fifteen from Mariupol. In all there were ninety-five of both genders. Baptize them with the fire of the Spirit, O Lord Jesus.

I presented all the articles of faith to the congregation in Neuendorf. The baptismal candidates sat on the front bench as was customary and I presented the customary questions which they answered with "yes." May the Lord Jesus seal that "yes" in all of them.

June 6

Our children the D. Epps returned to the community sheep farm. The Lord's angel go with them.

On Thursday Johann Braun and Johann Dyck Junior, both from Neu-Chortitza, appeared before the *Kirchenkonvent* charged with drinking strong liquor. They were admonished, made some promises to better themselves and were dismissed. The Lord grant them strength.

June 7

Our brother-in-law Jacob Stoess returned from visiting his friends.

June 8

This morning at 10 AM they left to return home. The Lord accompany him and his wife and children.

June 9

Elder Jacob Dyck baptized thirty-three persons of both genders in Neuendorf. "So neither he who plants nor he who waters is anything, but only God who makes things grow" [I Cor. 3:7]. I preached the preparatory sermon in Chortitza on Luke 14:23. Jacob Braun from Bergthal preached in Osterwick. Prepare us, Lord Jesus, so that we are worthy guests at your table.

June 11

Jacob Braun from Bergthal returned home after completing his business and visiting his friends. He visited us twice. The Lord's angel accompany you dear ones.

In the afternoon I preached the funeral service for the infant son of Jacob de Veer in Osterwick. He died on June 8 at 4 AM, at the age of three weeks and three days. Jesus accepts the children.

June 12

I travelled to the community sheep farm. They were making hay.

June 15

I returned safe and sound. Thank you, Lord Jesus. In the evening my cousin Cornelius Epp was here for a two-hour visit.

June 16

Elder Jacob Dyck celebrated holy communion with five hundred and eleven members of both genders in the Chortitza church. Jesus accepts sinners and eats with them. J. Regier preached the preparatory sermon in Neuendorf. Accompany these words with your blessing, Lord Jesus.

June 20

I preached the funeral sermon for our departed member, sister ? in Chortitza. She was ill for ten days. She died on June 18 at 7:30 PM. She reached the age of sixty-six years, five months and five days. Her first marriage lasted ? years. She gave birth to six sons and two daughters, of whom four sons and one daughter died. Her second marriage lasted seven years, two months and ? days. Her third marriage lasted nine years and twenty-seven weeks. There were no children from the last two marriages. The Lord was and is her true shepherd.

June 23

I preached the thanksgiving sermon after communion on Ephesians 1:3 in Chortitza. "Were not all ten cleansed? Where are the other nine?" [Luke 17:17]. In Neuendorf elder Jacob Dyck celebrated holy communion with members of both genders. The Lord is nigh to those who seek him. After our brother-in-law Thiessen and his wife took communion and visited their friends they began their return journey one June 26. The Lord's angel go with them.

June 29

I, David, Jacob, Heinrich, Johann and Bernd Rempel left for the annual fair in Yekaterinoslav.

July 2

We returned safely at 6 AM. Thank you, my Saviour, for your grace and love.

I preached the funeral sermon for our departed member, brother Cornelius Martens in the deceased's home in Einlage. He died on July 1 at 5 PM after an illness of fourteen days. He reached the age of sixty-one years, eight months and fourteen days. He was married for thirty-seven years, nine months and one day. He sired eleven children, of whom four died. He had fourteen grandchildren, of whom two died. Rest in peace, dear brother, until the end of days.

On June 30 Jacob Regier preached in Chortitza. H. Penner preached in Neuendorf, Johann Penner in Osterwick. Now thank we all our God, who wondrous things has wrought.

July 3

Our children, the Dick Epps, arrived from the community sheep farm and brought with them their infant son, David, who died on the evening of July 2. He was six weeks and four days old.

July 4

We held his funeral. Heinrich Penner preached the funeral sermon. Jesus accepts children.

July 5

Our children returned to the community sheep farm. My sister Anna also accompanied them. The Lord's angel guide you dear ones.

July 6

I and Johann Klassen from Kronsthal travelled to our community sheep farm. We returned safely on July 8 with my sister Anna. Thank you Lord Jesus.

July 7

Heinrich Penner from Schoenhorst preached [in Chortitza]. ? preached in Neuendorf. The Lord bless this [spiritual] seed to His glory.

Bruederschaft. The widow P. Dyck in Chortitza gave birth to a baby boy. She named the father as David Doerksen of Chortitza. He denied it, affirmed his innocence before the brethren and called on God as his witness. The matter was left to his conscience. Mrs Dyck was excommunicated from the congregation. God will bring to light what was hidden in darkness.

July 14

I preached on Revelation 3:20 in Neuendorf. H. Penner preached in Chortitza, Jacob Regier in Osterwick. May this seed fall on fertile ground.

July 16

In Nieder Chortitza I preached the funeral sermon for our departed member, sister Barbara Pankratz. She died on July 14 at 11 PM. after an illness of eleven weeks and three days in her fiftieth year of life. Her first marriage lasted half a year. Her second marriage lasted about thirteen years. She gave birth to ten children of whom four died. The dear Saviour grant you a gentle rest until the day of joyous resurrection.

July 21

Johann Dyck preached in Chortitza, Heinrich Penner Junior in Neuendorf. The Lord bless these messages.

July 28

Johann Dyck preached in Chortitza. Heinrich Penner Junior preached in Neuendorf, D. Wiens in Osterwick, ? in Rosengart. Bless these messages, O Lord Jesus.

Bruederschaft. The widow Mrs. Peter Dyck of Chortitza was accepted into the congregation by elder Jacob Dyck. She still insisted that Doerksen's son David (from Chortitza) was the child's father. The Lord "will bring to light what is hidden in darkness" [1 Cor. 4:5].

July 29

I preached the funeral sermon on ? for our departed member, brother Peter ? from Chortitza. He died from dropsy following a lengthy illness. His death occurred on July 27 at 10:30 AM. He reached the age of sixty-four years, eight months, four weeks and six days. His first marriage lasted approximately one year, the second four and a half years. Both marriages were childless. During his third marriage, which lasted seven and a half years, he sired four children, all of whom have died. His fourth marriage lasted twenty-six years and eight days. He sired two children, of whom one daughter is alive. He had one grandchild. The dear Saviour grant him rest (Matt. 11:28).

August 2

I preached the funeral sermon on ? for Helena, the deceased daughter of the miller Claas Wiebe of Chortitza. She died on July 31 at 10:30 AM following a ten-day illness. She reached the age of two years, eight weeks and six days. "Let the little children come to me and do not hinder them." [Mark 10:14]

August 4

Elder Jacob Warkentin from Altonau preached in Chortitza on Galatians 6: 7,8. A good sermon on Christian morality…? Wiensz preached in Neuendorf, in Osterwick Abraham Peters from Ladekop. The dear Saviour bless these messages to our salvation and to the honour of His name.

August 5

Elder Jacob Warkentin, H. Wiensz and Abraham Peters stopped by for coffee. They commence their return journey at 4:00 PM. The

Lord's angel accompany these dear people.

On Thursday the youth Michael Kaehler from Einlage appeared before the *Lehrdienst*. He and some others had destroyed vegetables in Jacob Hiebert's garden. All had been called before the local mayor. The others had admitted their wrongdoing, asked for forgiveness and reconciled with Hiebert. Kaehler did not do so. He had sworn and refused all correction. He was warned and told to better his ways. The problem could not be solved and will be presented to the congregation on Sunday. If he decides to reconcile with the offended party before then, the matter will be dropped. The brothers H. Hildebrand and Abraham Froese from Einlage were asked to deal with the matter. Lord, have mercy on him.

August 10

Elder Jacob Dyck preached in Chortitza on 1 Peter 2:21. Johann Dyck preached in Neuendorf, Heinrich Penner Junior in Osterwick. The grace of our Lord Jesus Christ be with us all.

Bruederschaft. Jacob Hiebert and Kaehler were reconciled in the presence of the brethren. It had not been possible earlier. Kaehler asked Hiebert and the congregation for forgiveness and it was granted. It was a shallow process, but according to protocol. It was a cermony which lacked true integrity.

In the afternoon I preached the funeral sermon for our deceased member, brother Claas Wiebe (the miller) from Chortitza. He emigrated from Prussia in 1839. He died on August 8 at 12 AM following an eleven-day illness. He reached the age of fifty-two years, eleven months and twelve days. He was married for twenty-three years, six months and six days. He sired eight children, seven of whom died. Rest in peace until the joyous resurrection.

August 17

Five young men arrived from Prussia in order to visit their friends. There was a Cornelius Jansz from Tiegenhof ?, a Wieler, a Pauls and two Wiens brothers. They spent the entire day with us. They continued their journey early in the morning.

August 18

I preached in Chortitza on ?. Johann Penner preached in

Neuendorf, Johann Dyck in Osterwick. Jesus, my desire and my salvation. Amen.

August 20

Our friends from Prussia began their journey to the Molotschna. The Lord's angel accompany them.

August 21

Elder Jacob Dyck and Heinrich Penner left for Bergthal to conduct a ministerial and deacon election. The dear Saviour bless their endeavours. In the evening our brother-in-law Heinrich Thiessen arrived with his wife and two children.

August 22

In the morning the Heinrich Thiessens and the Jacob Dycks left for Bergthal. The Lord's angel guide them there and back.

August 24

I preached the funeral sermon on Job 14: 1,2 at the David Wiensz residence in Kronstal for his little son Abraham. He died on August 22 at 7:30 AM after an illness of three days. He reached the age of one year, eleven months, five days. "Let the little children come to me and do not hinder them, for the kingdom of God belongs to such as these." [Mark 10:14]

August 25

I preached in Chortitza on Matthew 8:23-27. Jacob Regier preached in Neuendorf, Johann Dyck in Osterwick. "Lord, to whom shall we go? You have the words of eternal life." [John 6:68]

August 26

I, my wife and the children travelled to the sheep farm and returned safe and sound on August 29. Thanks to the Lord for his gracious protection.

August 27

My brother-in-law Heinrich Warkentin and his wife came for a visit. They ate lunch with us and then went to visit their friends.

August 28

Elder Jacob Dyck and brother Heinrich Penner returned from Bergthal. Brother J. Braun was elected elder; the deacon Peter Epp was elected as minister and brother Abraham von Bargen was elected as deacon—all were chosen by majority vote. May the Lord endow these men with the power of His Spirit.

August 30

Claas Wiensz from Kremenjchuk paid us a one-hour visit.

September 1

I preached in Neuendorf on Matthew 11:2. Brother H. Penner preached in Chortitza, elder Jacob Dyck in Osterwick. The Lord bless these messages. The Heinrich Warkentins Senior and the Peter Loewens had lunch with us. They left at 5 PM for the Island of Chortitza. The Lord's angel go with you dear ones.

September 3

The Heinrich Warkentins left at 5:30 AM on their return journey.

September 4

I and our son Jacob left for Yekaterinoslav in order to visit my brother-in-law Heinrich Thiessen.

September 5

I journeyed to Heinrich Gertz in Kronsgarten. In the afternoon he and I visited Mrs. F. Peters to inquire whether her daughter Susanna would accept a marriage proposal from our son Jacob. She accepted. Since Mrs Peters was separated from her husband, who is somewhat mad and living in the Molotschna, an immediate formal engagement seemed inappropriate and so was postponed for an indefinite period. I then visited the widow Mrs. Johann Klassen and Mr. Dirk Neufeld, had lunch with Mrs Peters and returned to Thiessens in Yekaterinoslav for the night.

September 7

We arrived home safely this evening. Thank the Lord for His gracious protection.

September 8

Elder Jacob Dyck preached in Chortitza on Revelation 2:2-6. Johann Dyck preached in Neuendorf, D. Wiensz in Osterwick. Lord Jesus, be gracious to us for the sake of Your great love.

Bruederschaft. Several young men from Einlage appeared before the *Lehrdienst* on September 7. They had stolen watermelons from the Russians, [were caught] and were arraigned before the [Einlage] mayor's office, where they were forced to pay twenty rubles in damages [to the Russians]. They were all excommunicated from the congregation. It is a very sad thing to deal with such people.

September 9

The H. Thiessens dropped by on their return journey from the Molotschna.

September 11

They continued their journey at 7 AM.

September 12

I presided at the marriage of Jacob Toews and Maria Dyck at the home of Aron Dyck in Chortitza. The Lord grant them a happy marriage.

Jacob Penner, the son of Johann Penner from Einlage, appeared before the *Lehrdienst*. He had made a human figure of straw, placed it on the street at night and set it ablaze. He tried to trivialize his action and make excuses. In the end he asked for forgiveness and made his peace.

September 15

I preached in Osterwick on Acts 4: 11-12. H. Penner preached in Neuendorf, Johann Penner in Chortitza. The Lord bless these messages.

September 19

Johann Friesen from Neuenburg appeared before the *Lehrdienst*. He had mistreated a Russian priest who had watered his horses [at Friesen's farmstead] without asking permission. He tried to justify his actions. The matter was referred to the *Bruederschaft*. The last to appear were Johann Driedger and Wilhelm Dyck and his wife, all from Blumengart. They had gathered wild honey in the Kamp without permission, then quarrelled with the watchmen Jacob Neufeld and Johann Wiensz. Mrs Dyck had hit Neufeld. They asked forgiveness and were reconciled. Lord, look upon us in mercy.

September 22

I preached in Osterwick on Isaiah 54: 1-3. Elder Jacob Dyck preached in Chortitza, H. Penner Senior in Neuendorf. You call, Lord Jesus, and I come to You weary and burdened. Help me. Amen.

Bruederschaft. Johann Friesen from Neuenburg was excommunicated from the congregation. The six young men from Einlage were readmitted into the congregation by elder Jacob Dyck. The district office had ordered them to do six days of public labour. It's all so ritualized. Since we do not possess the spirit of community we content ourselves with the dead letter of the law.

September 28

Jacob Stoess from Schoental came for a visit. They left for Neuendorf on September 29.

September 29

Johann Neufeld from Schoental preached in Chortitza on Luke 6:36. Abraham Peters preached in Neuendorf, H. Penner in Osterwick. Grant us all, O Lord Jesus, [a spirit of] genuine goodness.

October 1

This evening our children, Jacob, Lenchen and Heinrich left for Yekaterinoslav. Jacob travelled to Kronsgart to see his bride. The Lord's angel direct him.

October 2

Mr. and Mrs. Jacob Stoess left on their return journey. The Lord's angel go with them.

October 3

I presided at the marriage of Daniel Warkentin and Anna Friesen at the Jacob Warkentin residence in Rosengart. The Lord's blessing surround this marriage.

October 5

This evening our children returned from Yekaterinoslav and Kronsgarten.

October 6

I preached the harvest and thanksgiving sermon in Chortitza on Acts 14:17. Johann Penner preached in Neuendorf, D. Wiensz in Osterwick. Grant us a rich harvest of souls, Lord Jesus, and through your grace the eternal harvest of joy.

October 11

Elder Jacob Dyck together with Heinrich Penner and Jacob Regier returned home safe and sound this afternoon. He had installed Jacob Braun as elder in Bergthal. Thank God for His grace.

This evening the minister Abraham Sudermann from K ? in Prussia arrived here together with his family. They spent the night at Abraham Isaac's in Rosenthal.

October 12

In the afternoon they left to visit brother K. in Einlage.

October 13

David Wiensz preached in Chortitza on Matthew 22:34-40. Jacob Regier preached in Neuendorf, Johann Penner in Osterwick. Love covers a multitude of sins. Peter Bloch from Kronsgarten and Heinrich Pauls from Rosenthal were our guests.

Bruederschaft. Johann Friesen from Neuenburg was readmitted as a member of the congregation. Since we do not possess the power of the Spirit, we are content with the letter of the law.

October 23

Our daughter Catarina was inoculated against small pox by Peter ? . May the dear Friend of children make all things well. In the evening elder J. Braun from Bergthal visited us for one hour.

October 24

This morning elder J. Braun visited his friends, then left on his return journey. The Lord's angel accompany him.

In the afternoon I preached the funeral sermon on Job 14: 1,2 for our departed member Jacob Vogt from Chortitza. He died after an illness of eight days on October 22 at the age of fifty-eight years, two months, two weeks and one day. He was married for thirty-one years, one month and eighteen days. He sired fourteen children, of whom nine died. He had one grandchild who also died. Rest in peace dear brother until the end of days.

October 20

David Wiensz preached in Chortitza, Johann Dyck in Neuendorf and ? Penner in Osterwick. "Love is the fulfillment of the law" [Romans 13;10].

October 27

I preached in Nieder Chortitza on Luke 19:10. David Wiensz preached in Neuendorf, Jacob Regier in Osterwick, Jacob Dyck in Chortitza, Johann Penner in Rosengart. Jesus, You were born to seek what was lost.

Bruederschaft. Peter Reimer from Einlage admitted that he had an affair with the widow Mrs. Claas Peters while he was a married man. Both were excommunicated from the congregation.

October 28

I preached the funeral sermon on ? for our departed sister Maria Braun at the Dirk Braun residence in Einlage. She died on October 26 at 6:30 AM at the age of approximately fifty-seven years. Her first marriage lasted some ten years. She gave birth to five children, three of whom died. Her second marriage lasted twenty years, four months and twenty-four days. She gave birth to five children, two of whom died. She had seven grandchildren. Rest in peace dear sister and await the joyous resurrection after all your suffering.

October 31

I presided at the marriage of Julius Paetkau and Margareta Hildebrand at the H. Hildebrand residence in Burwalde. Grant your blessing to this union, Lord Jesus.

November 3

Jacob Dyck preached in Chortitza on Luke 10: 1,2. David Wiensz preached in Neuendorf, J. Regier in Osterwick. The Lord is near to the broken-hearted.

Bruederschaft. Peter Reimer and Mrs. Claas Peters were readmitted as members of the congregation by elder Jacob Dyck. Jesus accepts sinners.

November 8

Thursday. *Lehrdienst*. Peter Dyck from ? accused Wilhelm Zacharias from Osterwick and F. Thiessen from Neuendorf of keeping some of the monies from the sale of wool, and claimed Johann Braun from the *Chutor* still owed P.D. half the sum. Both declared they had not kept any money, had paid [Peter Dyck] and that he appeared to be satisfied with the payment. The dispute was not resolved.

There was another matter. Our brother-in-law's son, Peter Rempel, from Schoenhorst, is quarrelling with the village regarding a dam. The district office had ordered Rempel to open the dam so that the water could follow its normal course. Rempel did not wish to do so. He was advised to follow the directives of the district office. Finally he agreed to do so. Such disputes are not worth the effort.

November 9

I presided at the marriage of the widow Catarina Letkemann and the widower Daniel Wiebe. May the Lord's blessing rest upon them.

November 10

H. Penner Junior preached in Chortitza, Jacob Dyck in Neuendorf and D. Wiensz in Osterwick. Jacob Regier preached in Burwalde. May the dear Saviour bless these messages.

November 14

Thursday. The young men from Burwalde, Abraham Hiebert and ? , who did mischief during the night, had not followed the instructions of the mayor's office. Now they finally apologized. The matter was referred to the Sunday *Bruederschaft*. It seems that everyone wants to walk their own pathway.

November 17

H. Penner preached in Chortitza on 1 Timothy 6:12. Jacob Dyck preached in Neuendorf, D. Wiensz in Osterwick. O Lord Jesus, give me strength in the fight against sin. Amen.

November 21

Thursday. Harder from Thiessen's sheep farm accused Peter Peters from the *chutor* of having the French disease [venereal disease]. Peters was well. Harder apologized and the two were reconciled. "Watchman, what is left of the night?" [Isa. 21:11]

November 24

Johann Dyck preached in Chortitza on Psalm 119:32. H. Penner preached in Neuendorf, Jacob Dyck in Osterwick, David Wiensz in Nieder Chortitza.

Note: since the three youung men from Burwalde desperately pleaded for forgiveness the *Lehrdienst*, believing their promises to reform, decided not to present their names to the congregation. We sow in hope [of harvest].

November 26

I preached at the wedding of Jacob Toews and Anna Wiebe at the Peter Wiebe residence in Neuendorf. May the Lord Jesus grant this couple His blessing.

November 27

I preached the funeral sermon on ? for our departed member Johann Wieler in his home in Chortitza-Rosenthal. He was sick for twelve days with small pox ? and died on November 24 at 10 AM at the age of thirty-eight. He was married for eleven years, eleven months and three weeks. He sired two sons and one daughter, all of whom are alive. The dear Saviour grant him a gentle, blessed rest until the joyous day of resurrection for the elect.

December 1

Johann Dyck preached in Chortitza, Johann Penner in Neuendorf and Jacob Dyck in Osterwick. The Lord bless these messages.

December 8

Elder Jacob Dyck preached in Chortitza. Johann Penner preached in Neuendorf, David Wiensz in Osterwick, Jacob Dyck in Burwalde. May these messages produce fruit, O Lord Jesus.

Deccember 15

Elder Jacob Dyck preached in Chortitza on Rev. 22:12. H. Penner Senior preached in Neuendorf, H. Penner Junior in Osterwick. O that we could all say "Yes Lord Jesus, come quickly."

I preached the funeral sermon for a young man, Gottlieb Friedrich Seifert (a Lutheran), in Einlage. He was sick for four weeks. He died of a stroke on December 12 at 10 PM at the age of twenty-six.

December 17

I preached the funeral sermon for our departed member and sister in the home of Jacob Holzrichter in Chortitza. She died on December 12 at 9:45 PM following an illness of twenty-one weeks and five days. She reached the age of forty years, nine months and twenty-three days. She was married for eighteen years, ten months and eighteen days. She gave birth to eight children, of whom two died. She was the youngest daughter of the deceased elder Johann Wiebe. Jesus is "the resurrection and the life. He who believes [in Him] will live, even though he dies." [John 11:25]

December 19

I and our son Jacob travelled to Yekaterinoslav on business.

December 22

I preached in Chortitza on Zechariah 9:9. Elder Jacob Dyck preached in Neuendorf, H. Penner in Osterwick, H. Penner Junior in Nieder Chortitza. Be thou our refuge, Lord Jesus.

December 25

The first day of Christmas. I preached in Neuendorf on John 1:14. Elder Jacob Dyck preached in Chortitza on Luke 2: 8-14, ? in Osterwick, Johann Penner in ?. "Your word is a lamp to my feet and a light for my path." [Psa. 119:105]

December 26

On the second day of Christmas I preached in Chortitza on Jeremiah 9:6. Jacob Regier preached in Neuendorf, David Wiensz in Osterwick, H. Penner in Burwalde, Johann Penner in Rosengart. I know in whom I believe. Jesus is my salvation, my comfort, my hope.

December 29

The last Sunday of the year. I preached in Chortitza on Ephesians 2:22. Elder Jacob Dyck preached in Neuendorf. No one preached in Osterwick. O Lord Jesus, grant us grace to put aside all the sins which plague and make us weary.

This afternoon our children the Dietrich Epps returned to the sheep farm. Jacob accompanied them. They arrived here on December 25. God go with you dear ones.

Some Comments on the Year 1840

One hundred and fifty-seven males and one hundred and twenty-nine females—in all two hundred and eighty-six were born in the Chortitza and Schoenwiese districts. Sixty-one males and fifty-six females died—in all one hundred and seventeen. Births exceeded deaths by ninety-six males and seventy-three females—one hundred and sixty-nine in all. Fifty-eight people were married.

The winter was long and varied with up to 20.5° frost. Spring was late with much rain. Seeding was delayed. At first the winter rye showed little promise, then matured into a good harvest. The early summer brought storms and heavy rain. Hay and the grain crops did exceedingly well. The late summer and early fall were hot and dry. Late fall brought moderation and the rye germinated rather well. Snow and frost, with temperatures dropping to minus 20.5° began in mid-November. On November 9-20, with water levels being high, the Dnieper froze over.

Grain Prices. Wheat twelve to fifteen and one half rubles; rye twelve to seventeen rubles; oats five to seven rubles; millet eight to nine rubles; scotch barley twelve to thirteen rubles per *chetvert*. Butter costs thirty-two to forty-five kopecks; cheese thirty to thirty-eight kopecks; hay one hundred and twenty to one hundred and fifty rubles per load. Ewes six and a half to seven and a half rubles; cows forty-five to one hundred rubles; horses one hundred to two hundred and fifty rubles each.

The Kronsweide congregation built a church in Kronsweide. The foundation was of stone, the walls of brick. The monies came from the general fund. Elder Jacob Hildebrandt dedicated the structure on the Sunday before Christmas.

Congregational members are quarrelling among themselves and are at odds with their elder. May the dear Saviour grant the congregation his peace.

In our congregation we live according to the letter of the law. The Spirit is absent. Many words and few deeds. A teacher training school is to be built and the *Comitat* in Odessa has authorized a levy of six percent during this year. Some 30,000 rubles are to be raised for the school and for teachers' salaries.

In the Molotschna congregation the impact of the [church] split is being increasingly felt. The district office and the Agricultural Society rule more through despotism than through gentleness as Jesus taught. The fires of discontent glow under the ashes collectively and in all our churches. If a wind should drive the ashes away, the fire will become visible and the flames will be fanned. God have mercy on us.

Endnotes

[1] Epp's concern with the broken engagement probably reflects an older Prussian practice. Among the Prussian Mennonites an engagement celebration involved the extended families of both bride and groom and was regarded as an almost irrevocable pledge of marriage. Grooms who broke an engagement were considered poor marriage risks within the larger community.

[2] The hymnbooks issue is not clarified in Epp's diary. The January 26, 1840, entry suggests an application to approve their import.

[3] Epp documents the stupidity and deceit of his community in great detail. It must have required a strong sense of calling and a deep concern for righteousness to put up with such pettiness year in and year out.

[4] Village fires were not infrequent, especially in the early days of settlement when the use of thatch roofs was widespread. Since the barn was attached to the house, there was always the possibility of losing home, cattle, horses and farm inventory in a single conflagration. In such situations Epp does not doubt the love of Providence but does find it difficult to understand God's workings.

[5] Epp's concern with a "long neglected regulation" may refer to the use of the ban, practised over the centuries with varying degrees of severity. Its enforcement placed a member outside of the congregation and frequently curtailed both social and economic interaction with him/her. In a setting in which the interest of church and state were fused, as was the case in closed Russian Mennonite settlements, strict separation was difficult to enforce.

[6] The levy for the poor and for community expenses reflects the enmeshment of ecclesiastical and civil affairs in the self-governing Mennonite settlements. Both farmers and church members were taxed and the majority were active in both worlds.

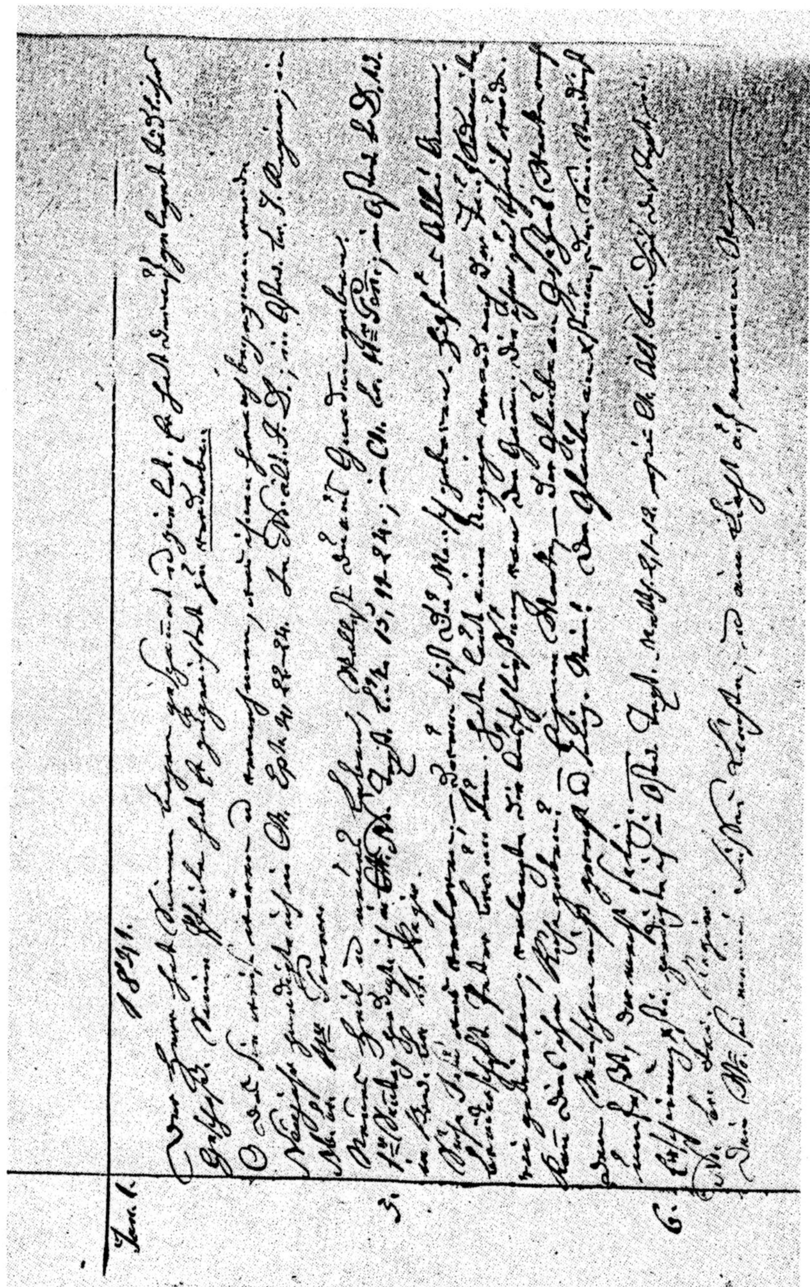

The first entries in Epp's 1841 diary.

1841

January 1

The Lord has bent His bow and is taking aim. He has placed in it a deadly missile. His arrows are intended to destroy. "If only they were wise and would understand this and discern what their end will be" [Deut. 32:29].

New Year's day. I preached in Chortitza on Ephesians 4:22-24. Elder Jacob Dyck preached in Neuendorf, J. Regier in Osterwick, J. Penner in Neuenburg.

By Your grace give us new life and new salvation.

January 3

On this first Sunday of the new year, I preached in Neuendorf on Luke 15:11-24. H. Penner preached in Chortitza, P. Dyck in Osterwick, J. Regier in Burwalde. Jesus, you became man to seek what was lost. Help us all. Amen.

Bruederschaft. Peter Braun Jr. who, according to report, had committed sodomy either before or after baptism, requested excommunication from the church. His request was granted. Will this bring him peace? Our own works do not make us righteous. No—faith in Christ and his work of redemption brings salvation.

January 6

Epiphany. I preached in Osterwick on Matthew 2:1-12. Elder Jacob

Dyck preached in Chortitza on the same text. J. Regier preached in Neuendorf. "Your word is a lamp to my feet and a light for my path" [Psa. 119:105].

Note: On January 5, I preached a funeral sermon at the Dirk Dyck residence in Rosenthal. The little baby died on December 31 at 10 PM at the age of five weeks and two days. "Let the little children come to me, and do not hinder them, for the kingdom of God belongs to such as these." [Mark 10:14]

January 12

I preached in Neuendorf on Matthew 6:9-13. H. Penner preached in Chortitza.

Bruederschaft. Peter Braun of Neuendorf was readmitted as a member of the congregation by elder Jacob Dyck. Jesus accepts sinners.

January 19

Johann Penner preached in Chortitza, H. Penner in Neuendorf, D. W. in Osterwick. May the Lord bless these messages.

January 24

I preached the funeral sermon at the Abraham Froese residence for his son Peter. He died on January 20 at 5 PM after an illness of ten days at the age of eleven years, six months and eighteen days. "Blessed are the dead who die in the Lord" [Rev. 14:13].

January 26

I preached in Osterwick on Acts 24:25. Johann Penner preached in Chortitza, H. Penner in Neuendorf. O dear Saviour, Holy Jesus, give us the strength for true repentance.

January 30

Thursday. Cornelius Wiebe appeared before the *Lehrdienst* in Burwalde. He was accused by Johann ? from Bergthal. At the Johann Fast residence in Einlage Wiebe had said that all the Mariupol settlers were thieves and cited certain [missing] cellar beams recorded by the son of the renter Fast. Wiebe could not or did not wish to remember. Wiebe was told to reconcile with both. The matter was taken under advisement.

Jacob W. from Schoenhorst was in conflict with members of the village office because of his nightly escapades. The matter was not resolved and demands further action.

The renter Unrau from Einlage claimed that the landholder Braun had stolen from him.

February 1

The dear brothers Peter Schmidt and Abraham Sudermann from Steinbach arrived here at lunch. Schmidt spent the night with us and Sudermann stayed with elder Jacob Dyck.

February 2

At 7 AM the dear brothers left for Yekaterinoslav. The Lord's angel accompany you.

I preached the preparatory sermon in Burwalde on Luke 14:24. Elder Jacob Dyck preached in Chortitza, H. Penner in Osterwick, Johann Penner in Neuendorf. O Jesus, prepare us for Your table.

February 3

I preached the funeral sermon for our departed member Wilhelm Peters. He died on January 30 at 2 PM after an illness of twelve weeks. He reached the age of forty-nine years, four months and eleven days. He was married for twenty-three years, seven months and fourteen days. He sired twelve children, three of whom died.

February 5

I preached the funeral sermon on ? for the baby Helena von Kampen at the Peter von Kampen residence in Neuenburg. She died on February 1 at 2 PM following a ten-day illness at the age of five and one-half months. Let the children come unto me.

February 9

I preached the preparatory sermon in Neuendorf on Luke 14:23. To you be the glory, Lord Jesus. Elder Jacob Dyck celebrated holy communion with two hundred and twenty-three members. "For whenever you eat this bread and drink this cup you proclaim the Lord's death until he comes" [1 Cor 11:26].

Elder Jacob Braun of Bergthal sent a written request for a loan of three thousand rubles to cover the cost of feed and fuel for those in need. Two of the brethren they sent, Johann Leydig and Falk from Bergthal, took charge of the three thousand rubles. The entire colony serves as the guarantee.

February 11

I presided at the wedding of the widow Maria Warkentin and the widower D. Braun in Einlage. I wish them a good marriage—which somehow I doubt.

Daniel Loewen from Neuhorst hanged himself. How sad and terrible.

February 16

Elder Jacob Dyck celebrated holy communion with two hundred and fifty-nine members in Neuendorf. I too was there as a guest. God be merciful to me as a sinner.

J. Regier preached the sermon of thanksgiving in Chortitza.

February 17

I and the H. Thiessens travelled together to Yekaterinoslav.

February 23

I preached the thanksgiving sermon in Rosengart after holy communion. Johann Penner preached in Neuendorf. J. Regier preached in Osterwick, H. Penner in Nieder-Chortitza, David W. in Chortitza. *Bruederschaft.*

February 25

The H. Thiessens and the widow Krahn left on their return journey. I preached the funeral sermon in the school house on Psalm 39:5. Sara Wieler was sick for two weeks and died on February 22 at 10 AM. She reached the age of two years, five months and twenty-one days. She, in all her innocence, went to be with the dear Saviour.

March 2

Jacob Dyck preached in Chortitza, David Wiens in Neuendorf, Jacob Regier in Osterwick. May the Lord bless [the messages].

March 7

I preached the funeral sermon at the Cornelius Peters home in Neu-Osterwick for the baby Cornelius Peters. He died on March 5 at 3 PM after a seven-day illness. He reached the age of thirty-five weeks and one day. Jesus accepts the children.

March 9

[Elder] Jacob Dyck preached in Chortitza, D. Wiens in Osterwick. Jesus' suffering and death shall be my liberation.

March 23

Palm Sunday. H. Penner Jr. preached in Chortitza on Matthew 24:1-3. D. Wiens preached in Osterwick.

March 28

On Good Friday elder Jacob Dyck preached on 2 Corinthians 5:21. Johann Dyck preached in Neuendorf, J. Dyck in Osterwick. Lord, I have done wrong. I am oppressed by a burden of sin. I have not walked the pathway you showed me. Lord Jesus, have mercy on me.

March 30

The first day of Easter. Elder Jacob Dyck preached in Chortitza on Mark 16:1-8.

J. D. preached in Neuendorf. I preached in Osterwick on Mark 16:1-8, Johann Penner preached in Rosengart, Jacob Regier in Nieder-Chortitza. The foundation of my faith rests on Jesus' resurrection.

March 31

The second day of Easter. I preached in Chortitza on Luke 24:13-36. H. Penner preached in Neuendorf, D. Wiens in Osterwick, Jacob Regier in Einlage. After my sermon I presided at the marriage of Franz Neufeld and the widow H. Dyck. I know that my Redeemer lives and He will keep me from all evil.

Bruederschaft. Peter Neufeld from Einlage who was excommunicated some time ago, is ill and desired readmission into the congregation. His request is presented to the brethren and approved. Peter Neufeld was readmitted by elder Jacob Dyck in the afternoon.

April 6

I presented the articles of faith in Neuendorf, using the text Romans 10:10. Elder Jacob Dyck did the same in Chortitza. Lord Jesus I believe, help my unbelief.

April 13

I [preached] in Neuendorf, elder J. Dyck in Choritza, ... J. Regier in Osterwick. Christ is my life and death my reward.

April 20

Around 8 AM this morning the H. Thiessens and their three children arrived from Yekaterinoslav for a visit. They had spent the night at the Aron Thiessens in Neuendorf in order to present their son Heinrich as a baptismal candidate. I presented the articles of faith for the third time, from item eight to the end. Elder Jacob Dyck did the same in Chortitza. In Neuendorf there were six male and twelve female candidates. Lord Jesus bless their intentions.

Bruederschaft. It was decided that if H. Heese from Ohrloff desired to take over the advanced school in Chortitza he could do so. Chortitza also agreed, but with greater debate. Lord Jesus guide everything to our best interest.

On Chortitza Island Johann Wiens desired to marry the sister of his deceased wife. The issue was presented to the congregation. Some objected but the majority remained silent. In the end nothing was decided. The matter was only discussed in Chortitza.

April 23

After the H. Thiessens had visited all their friends, they commenced their return journey at 8 AM. The Lord's angel accompany them.

April 27

I presented the articles one to nine for the fourth time. In Neuendorf there are eight male and fourteen female baptismal candidates. In Chortitza elder Jacob Dyck presented articles one to nine. Here there are fifty male and thirty-nine female candidates. Sanctify them through your grace, O Lord Jesus. Brother David Wiens preached in Osterwick.

May 4

I presented the articles of faith for the fifth time [in Neuendorf] Elder Jacob Dyck did the same in Chortitza. Write their names in the Book of Life God, in the Book of the Lamb slain for us.

May 6

Tuesday. Elder Jacob Dyck catechized the baptismal candidates in Chortitza, using the questions and answers in the first half of the catechism. Lord, you know them all. Be with them.

May 8

Ascension Day. I preached in Neuendorf on Mark 16:50-52. I catechized twenty-two candidates. The congregation was in a reverent mood. Elder Jacob Dyck preached in Chortitza and catechized ninety-two baptismal candidates. The congregation was restless. Lord have mercy on us.

Note. On April 6 Jacob Warkentin from Altonau and the deacon Johann Klassen of Ohrloff arrived at elder Jacob Dyck's home in Rosenthal. Johann Klassen was my guest for two hours on April 7. Both of them left on April 7. The Lord's angel accompany you, dear ones.

May 11

I catechized the Neuendorf baptismal candidates on the last part of the catechism. In Chortitza elder Dyck presented the articles for the sixth time and presented the essential questions to the candidates. The Lord bless all of them.

May 15

Thursday. Cornelius and H. Banmann and Peter Peters from the *chutor* were ordered to appear before the *Kirchenkonvent* of Chortitza and Schoenwiese. Peters was on a trip and did not appear. Peters had spread the rumour that the Banmann brothers were carrying on with Russian [women].

Isaak Rempel from Einlage appeared along with the Einlage mayor. He had transgressed village regulations. He was urged to comply with them and village authorities were requested to use tact. Our public order is in a sad state. We have good regulations but the power to enforce them is lacking.

May 16

Claas Wiens from Krementschug was our guest for a few hours this morning. His rental contract has expired. For the time being he plans to rent quarters in Halbstadt.

In the afternoon I preached the funeral sermon for baby Abraham, the son of the private school teacher Abraham V. in the home of Cornelius Pauls. He died after a five-and-one-half day illness at the age of thirty-three weeks and two days.

May 18

The first day of Pentecost. I preached on John 16:24-30 in ? before a well-attended assembly. H. Penner preached in Neuendorf, Jacob Regier in Osterwick, Johann Penner in Burwalde. The Lord Jesus bless these sermons. Amen.

May 19

Elder Jacob Dyck baptized ninety-two persons in the Chortitza church. I presented the articles in Neuendorf and presented the baptismal questions. Baptize them Lord Jesus with fire and the Spirit.

May 25

Elder Jacob Dyck baptized twenty-two candidates [in Neuendorf]. J. Regier preached the preparatory sermon in Chortitza. In the evening Claas Dyck and his son Cornelius came from ? with the hymn books. The Stoesz couple and their daughter Maria from Schoenthal also arrived.

May 27

This morning the Stoesz family and Claas Dyck left for Yekaterinoslav. An angel go with them.

Note: H. Heese was installed as the teacher in the [Chortitza] *Central Schule* by elder Jacob Dyck, D. Epp, H. Penner, Jacob Dyck, G. Vogt and Jacob Bartsch. The agreement is for one year at eight hundred rubles per year plus free housing and heating, free pasture for four cattle, two *pud* and eight loads of hay. Oh Lord Jesus may this all be for your honour and glory....

May 31

In the evening Johann Klassen and his son-in-law Johann Toews arrived from Halbstadt. They want to raise capital to build a factory. May the Lord bless this undertaking.

June 1

Elder Jacob Dyck celebrated holy communion with four hundred and sixty members in Chortitza. Holy Jesus be gracious to us for your Name's sake. Jacob Regier preached the preparatory sermon in Neuendorf.

Afternoon I preached the funeral sermon for little Johann, the son of widow Johann Wieler, at the home of the miller Aron Peters. He died on May 29 after a fourteen-day illness.

June 7

Johann Klassen and Baerg returned from Yekaterinoslav, had lunch with us and left at 2:30 PM to visit elder Jacob Dyck. They want to reach Schoenwiese by evening. The Lord's angel accompany you.

June 8

Elder Jacob Dyck celebrated holy communion with three hundred members in Neuendorf. H. Penner preached the sermon of thanksgiving in Chortitza. I did not attend the service because of illness.

June 9

In the afternoon elder Benjamin Dirks stopped here on his return journey with two other brothers. He had served the young people in Waldheim with holy baptism, presided over an elder election and reconciled elder Benjamin Wedel with his congregation. Elder Wedel withdrew a document in which he condemned the volost office for punishing a disobedient [colonist], then handing him over to the *Kirchenkonvent*. May the Lord make all things right. At 2:30 PM our dear guests continued their journey.

June 11

The H. Thiessens, the widow Krahn and her son Heinrich began their return journey [to Yekaterinoslav] after receiving holy communion. The Lord's angel go with you, dear ones.

June 15

Elder Jacob Dyck preached in Chortitza. H. Penner preached the sermon of thanksgiving in Neuendorf. J. Regier preached in Osterwick. Praise and thanks to You eternally, O Holy Jesus, for all Your mercies.

June 21

This evening Heinrich Heese from Ohrloff arrived here with his three children and moved into the home of Cornelius Pauls which had been reserved for them. His reception was without much fanfare. The school building is barely useable.

June 22

Johann Dyck preached in Chortitza. H. Penner preached in Neuendorf, Jacob Regier in Osterwick, D. Wiens in Nieder Chortitza. H. Heese visited me this afternoon. He was unhappy that the schooling question was not pursued more aggressively. Patience will be needed. May the dear Saviour grant it.

Note: On June 19 Abraham Neufeld from Einlage appeared before the *Lehrdienst*. In a letter to the volost office he accuses the mayor's office in Einlage of not punishing a number of offenses and there was some truth in what he said. Neufeld acknowledged that he was the author of the letter, admitted he had acted hastily and asked for forgiveness. The issue was referred to a decision of the *Bruederschaft* on June 24.

June 26

Elder Jacob Dyck had scheduled a meeting of the *Kirchenkonvent* at 2 PM at H. Penner's residence and invited the members of the district office and the *Waisenamt*. Elder Dyck and the members of the district office did not appear. No one knew why. We departed at 7 PM without finishing our business. Elder Jacob Dyck claimed he had forgotten. Thoughtlessness, carelessness—when will you stop?

June 28

I and my nephew Bernd Rempel travelled to Yekaterinoslav. We stayed with the H.. Thiessens. Around 6 PM I met my brother-in-law Thiessen at the merchant Kulobuchow's. He was drunk. He treated me like Simei treated David. Simei believed David had forced Saul's family from the throne and was responsible for killing the innocent males of Saul's family. Thiessen, incited by G. P. Schreiber, was angry that the school teacher Heese was joining the community. He believed that his father-in-law had been wrongly treated by the commission investigating crown monies and finances. My conscience is clear . . . I forgive him. This is the third incident in four years. The first time I was offended. The second time I thought it was of the Lord. He gravely insulted his brother-in-law Siemens and forbade him to stay at his house. Siemens left the next morning. Some say Siemens had it coming. Let the Lord judge. We arrived home safely on July 1. Thank God for his gracious leading.

June 29

Elder Jacob Dyck preached in Chortitza. We held a general *Bruederschaft*.

1. Six single men were excommunicated from the church because of their inappropriate lifestyle.

2. Abraham Neufeld of Einlage was pardoned without having to appear before the brethren. The Einlage village council apologized to the congregation and was forgiven.

3. The brethren authorized the collection of money by Johann Klassen of Halbstadt for the construction of the factory.

4. Working or hauling wood on Sundays and holidays was strongly discouraged.

5. The brethren were warned against inappropriate behaviour at the annual fairs. If it occurs the *Lehrdienst* should be informed.

6. Minors who invite punishment through naughty behaviour shall be corporeally punished by their parents or guardians in the mayor's or district office when it is deemed appropriate.

7. G. Rempel, who was at odds with the local mayor's office, apologized and reconciliation took place.

The *Bruederschaft* ended peaceably at 3 PM. Will these resolutions be carried out? Will we have the resolve to do so? Lord be with us for Jesus' sake.

July 2

I, H. Penner and Jacob Regier received a written invitation to appear before elder Jacob Dyck at 2 PM. It was 5:30 PM when I received the letter. Since I was still weak [from illness?] I stayed home. What is going on? We seem to be groping in the dark. But He [God] will make all things well.

At the end of the month elder Jacob Braun from Bergthal stopped by to see elder Jacob Dyck. He wanted advice. The daughter of Cornelius Friesen had an affair with the young man Siemens and gave birth to a child. It was murdered and found dead on the manure pile. Apparently both her parents and the Siemens were aware of what happened. They were excommunicated from church. Elder Jacob Dyck advised him to report the perpetrators to the authorities. O Lord, have mercy on us. This is the first infanticide since the Mennonites migrated to Russia. How horrible!

July 6

Johann Dyck preached in Chortitza, H. Penner Jr. in Neuendorf, J. Dyck in Osterwick.

July 7

Monday. A joint meeting of the *Kirchenkonvent* and the members of the district office was held at H. Penner's residence in Chortitza. The members of the school commission were elected. The chairpersons are H. Penner and Jacob Regier; associate chairperson is Johann Penner of Rosenthal; the treasurer is Johann Siemens of Rosenthal. The statutes of the school were approved with the possible exception of the planting of fruit trees, proposed as a learning project for the youngsters. The chairperson was charged with formalizing the statues and school contract and presenting them to the *Kirchenkonvent* for approval. May the Lord bless all these endeavours.

July 9

Peter Schmidt from Steinbach arrived here in the evening and continued his journey to R.

On Thursday the secretary G. Penner appeared before the *Kirchenkonvent* regarding his drinking, swearing and blasphemy of the Saviour. He confessed his shortcomings and promised to better himself. May the Lord Jesus grant him deep repentance.

On July 7 J. Penner of Schoenhorst was mandated to invite Wilhelm Rempel from the *chutor* before the *Lehrdienst* for drunkenness in Tamakova. No one appeared and no reason was given.

July 12

I preached the funeral sermon on ? in the home of Johann Hiebert for his daughter Elisabeth. She died on July 10 at 6 PM after an illness of seven days at the age of five years and seven months. Jesus accepts the children.

July 13

Elder Jacob Dyck preached in Neuendorf. In the afternoon there was a funeral. I preached the funeral sermon at the Johann ? residence for his daughter Catarina. She died after an eight-day illness on July 11 of 7 PM. She reached the age of three years less two days. The father was very drunk.

July 19

I preached a funeral sermon in the home of Bernd Rempel for his mother, the widow Margareta Rempel. Her illness, which began with a stroke, lasted five years, seven months and seven days. She was a widow for twenty years, two months and sixteen days. While married she bore six sons and five daughters. Four of her sons are alive. She had nineteen grandchildren, of whom sixteen are alive. Peace to her ashes and rest for her weary soul.

July 20

I was finally able to attend the church service in Chortitza. Illness had prevented me from doing so since June 4. Elder Jacob Dyck preached on Hebrews 12:12-14. H. Penner Jr. preached in Neuendorf, J. Dyck in Osterwick. Thanks be to God for His love and faithfulness to me. In the afternoon I preached a funeral sermon at the home of the tenan [*Anwohner*]. Johann W. His little son died on July 18 at 10 PM, as a result of dysentery at the age of three years, six months and twenty days. He was sick for three days. Blessed are the dead who die in the Lord.

July 25

I preached the funeral sermon for Margareta the daughter of my brother-in-law, Johann Klassen of Blumengart. She died on July 23 at 7 PM after an illness of six days. She reached the age of one year, eight months, twelve days and twenty-one hours. Jesus accepts the children.

July 26

I preached in Chortitza on Matthew 5:6. Elder Jacob Dyck preached in Neuendorf, H. Penner in Osterwick, Johann D. in Nieder Chortitza.

O Lord, grant us all a true hunger for You.

August 3

I preached in Chortitza on Luke 19:10. Elder Jacob Dyck preached in Neuendorf, H. Penner Jr. in Osterwick, J. Dyck in Nieder Chortitza.

August 4

I preached the funeral sermon on ? at the Cornelius Martens residence in Einlage. Little Cornelius was sick for twelve days and died on August 3 at 3 AM, at the age of one year, two months and thirteen days.

August 6

I preached the funeral sermon on Hebrews 13:14 for our deceased member Bernd Klippenstein. He died on August 4 at 12:30 PM after an illness of three and a half days. He had small pox on his left side. He reached the age of sixty years, three months, three weeks, and four days. He was married for thirty-six years and one month. He sired twelve children, of whom seven died. He had twenty-two grandchildren, of whom six died. Rest gently in your [eternal] inheritance.

August 7

Peter [Gerbrandt] appeared before the *Kirchenkonvent* on Thursday. The daughter of Isaak Klassen accused him of raping her, which he vehemently denied. The matter was referred to the brethren on Sunday. The Lord will bring to light what is hidden in darkness.

Note: On August 6 the Minister of Imperial Domains, Kiselev, journeyed through Neuenburg on his way to Taganrog. Elder Jacob Dyck and district head J. Bartsch awaited him at the Jacob Krahn residence.

Since the minister spoke only Russian the district secretary G. Penner served as translator. The minister was not very happy with the forest plantations.[1] Apparently the Guardian's Committee [*Comitaet*] will cease to be and the colonies will be placed directly under government control. May the Lord make all things well.

August 10

I preached in Neuendorf on Matthew 5: 13-17. H. Penner preached in Chortitza, Johann Penner in Osterwick, Johann Dyck in Burwalde. May we all, Lord Jesus, stand as shining lights.

August 17

I preached in Neuendorf on Acts 3:20. H. Penner preached in Chortitza, David Wiensz in Osterwick. The Lord is my salvation. In him will I trust.

Bruederschaft. The daughter of Isaak Klassen and Peter Gerbrand, who were excommunicated on August 10, were readmitted by elder Jacob Dyck. Gerbrand had denied the deed until August 16, then confessed. O Lord, have mercy upon us.

In Neuendorf Johann Dyck and the widow Tilitzky were excommunicated on August 10 for adultery. Mrs. Tilitzky gave birth to a child. When will it all end?

August 20

I preached the funeral sermon on ? for Anna, the daughter of Peter Reimer of Einlage. She died yesterday at 4 PM after a ten-day illness (dysentery) at the age of seven years, three months and fifteen days. This child too went to be with Jesus.

August 23

I preached in Osterwick on Matthew 5:13-16. Johann Penner preached in Chortitza, H. Penner in Neuendorf.

August 24

Our children Diedrich Epp and his wife, Jacob, Helena and Johann left today at 2 PM to visit their friends [in the Molotschna]. They want to spend the night with Martin Schmidt in Schoenwiese.

August 31
I preached in Osterwick on Matthew 20:29-34. Johann Penner preached in Chortitza, H. Penner in Neuendorf. The Lord is my portion, says my soul.

September 3
Our children returned from the Molotschna. Thank the Lord for his protection. Friends from Altonau accompanied them—Cornelius, Penner, Bernd, Warkentin and their wives.

September 5
[Our guests] left for Yekaterinoslav. Our children the Epps left for their sheep farm at 4 AM. The Lord go with you, dear ones.

September 7
I preached in Burwalde on John 1:17. Jacob Regier preached in Chortitza, Johann Penner in Neuendorf, J. Penner Senior in Osterwick. We do not become righteous through the works of the law but through faith in Jesus Christ.

Bruederschaft. J. Unrau of Neu-Kronsweide was excommunicated for drinking and theft. May the Lord have mercy on him.

On September 4 there was *Kirchenkonvent* in Chortitza. Peter Heide and Peter Epp of Bergthal and other parties with disputes were heard. All the quarrels were resolved. "Teach us to number our days aright, that we may gain a heart of wisdom" [Psa. 90:12].

September 9
Our Molotschna friends returned from Yekaterinoslav safe and sound and stayed with the J. Dycks. I presided at the marriage of David Klassen and Anna Penner at the Johann Penner residence in Blumengart. The Lord bless this couple.

September 10
This evening the H. Thiessens, Johann Bergen and the widow Krahn arrived from Yekaterinoslav.

September 11
This afternoon our Molotschna friends began their return journey

travelling as far as Schoenwiese.

September 13

Today is my sixtieth birthday. You, dear Saviour, have led me all this time like a father. Praise and thanks for all I have received, for all benefits, testings, pain and suffering. Guide me until the end of my days. Then when no friend or brother can comfort me, guide me through the dark region of death unto eternal joy. Do this, O Lord Jesus, for the sake of your eternal love. Amen.

September 14

J. Regier preached in Chortitza on I Peter 5:11,12. Johann Penner preached in Neuendorf, H. Penner Senior in Osterwick. God's grace is abundant. After the sermon Jacob Regier presided over the marriage of Johann Sawatzky and Helena Enss, both from Osterwick. May the Lord's blessing rest upon this couple.

Bruederschaft. The old Jacob Wiens from Osterwick who is ill, confessed that he had committed sodomy in his youth and while a widower had committed adultery with a Lutheran woman. He was excommunicated from the congregation. May he not rely on external liturgies, but focus on Jesus and find his refuge in true faith. Seek Jesus and his light. Nothing else avails.

September 21

David Wiens preached in Chortitza on Matthew 22:30-34. J. Regier preached in Neuendorf, Johann Penner in Osterwick, H. Penner in Nieder Chortitza. Love ends the rule of law.

Bruederschaft. Jacob Wiens of Osterwick was accepted as a member of the congregation by elder Jacob Dyck. Jesus accepts sinners.

September 23

I presided at the marriage of the teacher J. Dyck of Chortitza and Katarina Siemens. The Lord's blessing rest upon this couple. Elder Jacob Braun and his wife from Bergthal arrived at the Peter Braun residence in Chortitza this evening.

September 26

Rev. Peter Epp from Heubuden, [Prussia] visited us for several hours.

September 28

David Wiens preached in Chortitza. Jacob Regier preached in Neuendorf, elder Jacob Braun from Bergthal in Osterwick. Love covers a multitude of sins.

This afternoon I presided at the marriage of Abraham van Bergen and Helena Dyck at the Einlage residence of Abraham Dyck.

October 2

Her imperial majesty the grand duchess Helena Pavlovna and her daughter Maria Michailovna travelled through Einlage to Yekaterinoslav via Neuendorf. They arrived at 3:15 PM. The grand duchess was very friendly and accepted a thank you speech and the good wishes presented by elder Jacob Dyck. She spoke with the private school teacher Hausknecht whose pupils sang in French for the grand duchess until she stepped out of her boat. She spoke ? with the teacher H. Heese concerning the *Zentralschule* and accepted a plan of the school building and a sketch [of the building] from his daughter Agata. Without stopping anywhere else the high-born travellers continued their journey escorted by eight corsairs [*Corossen*]. The Lord's angel go with them.[2]

October 4

Elder Jacob Braun from Bergthal spent several hours visiting us.

October 5

In Chortitza elder Jacob Braun preached a harvest sermon on Jer 5:24-25. D. Wiens preached in Neuendorf, Jacob Regier in Osterwick. Give us a good harvest, O Lord Jesus.

Bruederschaft. J. Unrau from Neu Kronsweide was accepted as a brother in the congregation. The Lord be with him for the sake of His merciful love.

The nephew of my wife, the youth H. Thiessen, died at 12:20 PM following an illness of ten days. At the end he suffered from apoplexy for fourteen hours. The dear Saviour atone for his youthful failings and shortcomings for the sake of his great love.

October 7

My sister-in-law Thiessen and the widow Krahn arrived at the Dyck residence for the funeral.

October 9

Martin Penner of Rosengart appeared before the *Kirchenkonvent* on account of his drinking. He pled not to appear before the congregation. He would do so [in the future] if he failed to stop drinking. Elder Jacob Dyck recommended he be given a second chance and all agreed. May the Lord grant him the insight to better himself.

Abraham Hiebert and his wife from Einlage are also to appear. They have quarrelled and separated. He is living on a *chutor* with a Russian woman. She tried to explain herself. He did not make an appearance. The matter was deferred for congregational discernment on Sunday.

In the afternoon I preached the funeral sermon for the deceased youth H. Thiessen at my brother-in-law Dyck's. He died after a ten-day illness at the age of eighteen years, four months and eighteen days. The dear Saviour will be gracious to him.

The son-in-law of Johann Klassen of Halbstadt, a certain ? , arrived here to collect the ? as our contribution to the building of the factory. May the Lord bless him.

October 12

[Elder] Jacob Dyck preached in Chortitza. David Wiens preached in Neuendorf, Jacob Regier in Osterwick, I in Einlage.

Bruederschaft. Abraham Hiebert failed to appear before the congregation. He has been rescheduled to appear next Sunday. All is vanity.

In the afternoon H. Penner of Prangenau as well as the young man H. ? of Blumenort were our guests.

October 14

I, our children the D. Epps and the Hienrich Penners of Prangenau left for our community sheep farm.

October 16

The Penners returned as far as Chortitza and left for the Molotschna the next day. The Lord's angel accompany these dear ones.

October 18

I got home safe and sound. Thanks be to the dear Saviour.

October 19

H. Penner Jr. preached in Chortitza. Jacob Dyck preached in Neuendorf, D. Wiens in Osterwick, J. Regier in Nieder Chortitza.

Bruederschaft. Hiebert promised that he will live together with his wife in the future. The congregation accepted his promise and he left in peace. They [the congregation] acted contrary to God's Word. Such a person is an adulterer, etc. and still calls himself a brother. We should have nothing to do with him.

October 25

I preached the funeral sermon on ? for our member Anganeta Wall in Neuhorst. She died of apoplexy two and one-half days after giving birth to a healthy daughter. She reached the age of nineteen years, two weeks and six days. She was married for one year less six weeks. She died at 6 PM on October 22. The Lord will be gracious to her soul. In the evening Abraham Klassen from Schoenhorst visited us for a few hours. I lent him two rubles ? for [the purchase of] a church [record] book.

October 25

Abraham Klassen from Schoenthal preached in Chortitza on Isaiah 66:2. J. Dyck preached in Neuendorf, D. Wiens in Osterwick Jacob Regier in Nieder Chortitza. "A bruised reed he will not break" [Isa. 42:3].

October 30

Johann Hiebert from Kronsweide appeared before the *Kirchenkonvent* meeting in the Chortitza church. He is spending too much time with Cornelius F., who was excommunicated from the Kronsweide congregation. He acknowledged his wrongdoing, asked for forgiveness and left, having made his peace. This is the first case of this nature under elder Jacob Dyck's leadership. Will this kind of vigilance be exercised in the future?

November 2

John Dyck preached in Chortitza, H. Penner in Neuendorf, David Wiens in Osterwick. The Lord's blessing rest upon these messages. Today our son Jacob was engaged to Maria Klassen from [Chortitza]. The

Lord's blessing rest upon them.

On November 1 the engaged couple Johann ? and the widow Wiebe who had twice been announced to the congregation decided to call off their engagement. Will elder Jacob Dyck continue to tolerate these and other cases like them?

November 6

The Chortitza *Kirchenkonvent* and the Schoenwieser *Konvent* met jointly. Abraham Penner from ? rental land and Abraham Janz, employed by Daniel Peters, appeared on charges of attempting to steal rye at Peters' [farm]. Wilhelm Bergmann caught them in the act. Janz admitted to this and a number of other planned thefts. Penner wanted to blame Janz. The matter was deferred to Sunday for action by the brethren.

Gerhard Friesen, separated from his wife, is spending all his time with the widow Mrs. Peter Dyck in Chortitza and, as could be expected, both admitted to living in adultery. Both were admonished and he was ordered to live in another village. He promised to do so. "Watchman what of the night" [Isa. 21:11].

November 9

J. Dyck preached in Chortitza on Acts 22:14. H. Penner preached in Neuendorf, Jacob Dyck in Osterwick. "Blessed and holy are those who have part in the first resurrection." [Rev. 20:6]

Bruederschaft. Abraham Penner was excommunicated from the congregation. The Lord have mercy on him.

November 15

At the request of the *Kirchenkonvent* I, G. Schreiber and G. Penner went to Tomakovka to talk with the daughter of Class Krahn in Schoenthal. She had served at Julius Janz's in Einlage, carried on with a Russian, got pregnant and gave birth to a son. She secretly left the colony prior to the birth. We stopped at the local constable's office, but he was not at home. The local priest had also left. We went to the second priest, by the name of ? and presented our concerns to him. We namely wished to speak with the girl and hear what she had decided to do. He gladly accommodated our wishes and sent a messenger to her that she appear immediately. The priest declared that he had twice written to the Consistorium and now the Consistorium had written to the Guardian's Committee [*Comitaet*]. Nothing could be done until a reply was received. He did say her son had been baptized. He had a request. Would we be able to provide a document stipulating that she had no record of theft or other criminal activity? If so, the clergy of the orthodox church would be free to accept her. Krahn appeared. After some introductory comments I asked her if she was joining the Russian [Orthodox] Church of her own free will. She answered "yes." Had she thought about this step and weighed the consequences? She answered, "For a long time." Did she know what sorrow this would cause her parents? She answered that her parents had long known about this. Question: From what you have told the priest you have requested a document of transfer. To whom did you apply? She was silent. We told the priest that she was inclined to join the Russian Church. We returned home. I had predicted it was too late. The fault lies with our spiritual and secular officials. We'll hear more cases of the same.

November 16

Elder Jacob Dyck preached in Chortitza. Johann Dyck preached in Neuendorf, J. Penner in Osterwick, D. Wiens in Burwalde. Blessed rather are those who hear God's Word and obey it. I was at the H. Funks in Schoenwiese at the engagement of our neighbour's son Gerhard Loewen and Anganeta Funk. May the Lord accompany this couple with his blessing.

November 17

I, the neighbour David Loewen and his wife returned safely. Thank you, Saviour.

November 18

Our son Jacob and his bride Maria Klassen were married at the residence of our next door neighbour Peter Klassen. Elder Jacob Dyck presided. The Lord's blessing rest upon their marriage spiritually and materially. Amen.

November 20

Thursday. Johann Brand from Schoenhorst and the widow Wiebe from Chortitza appeared before the *Kirchenkonvent*. They had agreed to be married and were publicly announced twice, but then separated. In the presence of the *Kirchenkonvent* Brand agreed to pay his former bride thirty rubles, the amount she demanded. They parted in peace. This is another one of these bad decisions by the *Konvent* which will have its consequences.

November 21

My sister Anna Epp moved into her new residence with the widow P. Enss of R. She lived with us for four years. I wish her greater tranquillity and I think she will find it there if she follows my advice. The dear Saviour, who gives power to the weak, will give her the strength to follow through.

November 23

Elder Jacob Dyck preached in Chortitza on Act 22:12. H. Penner preached in Osterwick, J. Dyck, in Neuendorf. "Behold I come soon" is a call to all of us. Lord Jesus, make me ready.

November 27

Abraham and Peter Klassen and Herman Schapansky from Burwalde appeared before the *Kirchenkonvent* on Sunday. The first two had been drinking at the pub of Abraham Bartsch and got into a fight. Abraham Klassen had to be bound and placed under guard.

P. Klassen wanted to free his brother but did not succeed. Schapansky was completely drunk but remained calm. The first two claimed ignorance. Schapansky asked for forgiveness and promised to better himself. The matter was deferred to the brethren on Sunday. O what great indifference and madness!

November 30

The first Sunday in advent. I preached in Chortitza on Zechariah. 9:9. Elder Jacob Dyck preached in Neuendorf, Johann Dyck in Osterwick, Johann Penner in Rosengart. Come, O Lord Jesus, prepare us.

Bruederschaft. Peter and Abraham Klassen were excommunicated from the congregation. Schapansky was forgiven by the brethren. Gerhard Froese, who is carrying on with the widow Mrs. Peter Dyck and rejects all admonishment, was excommunicated from the congregation. What great blindness! Abraham Penner from *chutor* was accepted as a member of the congregation. Will it help him?

December 1

This afternoon at 2 PM the dear brother Abraham Isaak arrived from Tiege accompanied by his driver, H. Dyck of Lindenau. The daughter of Peter Guenter of Rueckenau was with them. Catarina Guenter, aged eighteen and half, suffers from mental illness. It began two years ago and has steadily gotten worse. It apparently resulted from a [broken] love affair. She is to be taken to the doctors in Yekaterinoslav. The Lord grant his blessing.

December 2

Our dear friends continued their journey at 8 AM. I presided over the marriage of Gerhard Loewen and Anganeta Funk of Schoenwiese. The wedding took place at the H. Funk residence. The Lord's blessing accompany the couple.

December 4

I presided at the marriage of Gerhard Rempel and the widow Catarina Wiebe at the residence of the carpenter Abraham Dyck of Einlage. The widow was once a Lutheran but had been accepted into the Schoenwiese congregation through water baptism by elder Jacob Hildebrand. She came over to us, was twice presented to the congregation without the customary question being asked, even though I reminded elder Jacob Dyck of this. May the Lord bless this couple.

December 7

Second Sunday in advent. I preached in Chortitza on Revelation 1:7-8. Jacob Regier preached in Neuendorf, Johann Dyck in Osterwick.

Bruederschaft. Johann Penner had an affair with the daughter of Peter Reimer. She bore a child. Both were excommunicated from the congregation. Have mercy on us, [O Lord]!

December 14

Third Sunday in advent. I preached in Schoenhorst on Psalm 24:9-10. H. Penner preached in Chortitza, D. Wiens substituted for elder

Jacob Dyck in Osterwick. Johann Dyck preached in Nieder Chortitza. O Lord Jesus, prepare our hearts to receive you.

Bruederschaft. Peter and Abraham Klassen were readmitted into the congregation by elder Jacob Dyck. When the power of the Word is no longer there we succumb to legalism. Lord, have mercy on us.

December 21

Fourth Sunday of advent. Johann Penner preached in Chortitza, J. D. preached for me in Neuendorf. D. Wiens preached in Osterwick for elder Jacob Dyck. O Lord Jesus, prepare us to be born anew.

Bruederschaft. The daughter of Peter K. and Johann Penner were readmitted as members of the congregation.

December 25

The first day of Christmas. Johann Penner preached in Chortitza on Luke 2. I preached in Osterwick on John 1:14. H. Penner preached in Neuendorf, Jacob Regier in Neuenberg, elder Jacob Dyck in Burwalde, D. Wiens in Einlage.

December 26

I preached in Chortitza on Jeremiah 8:14. H. Penner preached in Neuendorf, D. Wiens in Osterwick, Johann Penner in Rosengart. So end the festive days. Thank you, O Lord Jesus.

December 28

The last Sunday of the year. J. Regier preached in Chortitza, Johann Penner in Neuendorf, H. Penner in Osterwick. I was asked to go to Nieder Chortitza, but no one there knew of any arrangements so I went home. Soon my last hour will come. Lord Jesus prepare me for a blessed departure.

December 31

In our local community one hundred and thirty-seven males and one hundred and seventy-six females were born. Ninety males and eighty-three females died. One hundred and forty more were born than died.

Congregational life. Immorality seems to have the upper hand.

Adultery, unethical behaviour, dances at weddings, and annual fairs — all this seems to be the order of the day. Separation from the congregation is supposed to control ethical behaviour. There is no thought of repentance and conversion. Little attention is paid to spiritual life. What the Spirit of God says can be literally applied, "You have a reputation of being alive but you are dead" [Rev. 3:1].

A *Zentralschule* has been built, thanks to the insistence of the teacher Heinrich Heese. Who is to pay for the cost of the building— the congregation or the general treasury? As yet we don't know. Praise God the school standards are rising.

Higher authorities wish to curb the immoral lifestyle in the congregations. The district books are to be circulated, the names of the immoral members entered and their transgressions as well as punishments listed. Why is this happening? Because we do not enforce our own regulations through church discipline. Like wild elephants that are being captured we are surrounded by strong palisades. May we, like David, have our eyes on the Lord from whom comes our help. "Do I take any pleasure in the death of the wicked?" [Ezek. 18:23]. I will redeem you and set you free. Yes, Lord Jesus, in your grace have mercy on us.

Things are very unsettled among the Molotschna congregations. Elder J. Warkentin, because of unwise actions, finds himself in great difficulty. Higher authorities have subjected him to other elders, which in turn presents them with a serious dilemma. May the Lord redeem them from all evil. He will redeem them and bring them together in unity.

The spring and early summer were productive. The summer was hot and dry. The winter rye produced well. Some of the summer grains did well, others poorly. It was an average hay crop. Rye sold for ten to twelve rubles per *chetverik*, wheat fourteen rubles, barley and oats seven to eight [rubles], millet eight rubles per *chetverik*. Hay sold for two hundred and fifty rubles per load. Wool sold at nineteen rubles, twenty-five kopecks per *pud*. Sheep and rams sold at four to six rubles each. There was no market for horses and cattle. Butter sold for twenty-five to thirty kopecks per pound, lard nine to ten rubles per *pud*. The winter rye sprouted nicely in fall, since it was moist and wet.

There were frequent reports of earthquakes, hail, heavy rains and hurricanes.

The rod which will correct us has already been bound. In the south and the east there are threatening clouds on the political horizon which threaten to engulf us. See Wisdom of Solomon [Apocrypha] Chapter 5. "Why are you downcast, O my soul? . . . Put your hope in God" [Psa. 42:5]. He is your helper. Have mercy, O Lord Jesus, for the sake of your great love. Amen.

Endnotes

[1] The Minister of State Domains, General Count P.D. Kiselev, seems to have known the Mennonites well and was impressed with their farming and governance practices. He was concerned with the plight of Russia's state peasants, which constituted about fifty-percent of the peasant population. All foreign settlers also came under Kiselev's authority. The early August visit constituted a high honour for the religious and civil leaders of Chortitza.

[2] Epp refers to the visit of the German-born Grand Duchess Elena Pavlovna and her daughter Maria Michaelovna. The welcome by elder Jacob Dyck; Mennonite school children singing a French song under David Hausknecht's direction; Heinrich Heese anxiously displaying blueprints for the proposed *Zentralschule*; the military pomp of the escorting horsemen proceeding through the peaceable Mennonite village of Einlage—all this must have constituted the central theme of village gossip for months to come.

1842

If something is to succeed, begin with prayer. One cannot be arrogant in such a crucial endeavour.

January 1

New Year's day. This Thursday elder Jacob Dyck preached in Chortitza, H. Penner Jr. in Neuendorf, H. Penner Senior in Osterwick. O Lord Jesus, give us strength to resist our sinful inclinations.

January 6

On January 4 David Wiens preached in Chortitza, Jacob Regier in Neuendorf, Johann Penner in Osterwick. Enlighten us all with your Holy Spirit. I witnessed the blessing of the waters in Yekaterinoslav. What superstition and vain action!

January 11

Jacob Dyck preached in Chortitza, David Wiens in Neuendorf, J. Regier in Osterwick, Johann Penner in Nieder Chortitza.

January 12

I travelled to our sheep farm. During the Christmas holidays fire broke out among the hay stacks around 3 PM but it was immediately discovered and extinguished.

January 14

I discovered the culprits [who set the fire]. They apologized and promised never to do it again. I forgave them with all my heart. If the hay alone had burned it would have meant a fifteen-hundred-ruble loss. In all we would have needed at least three thousand rubles to feed the animals. While I was there and on the way home I suffered from rheumatic fever. I arrived home ill on January 17. My God will work things out as they are best for me.

January 18

Jacob Dyck preached in Chortitza, David Wiens in Neuendorf, Jacob Regier in Osterwick. May God bless all.

January 24

Elder Jacob Dyck visited me on Saturday. O God, he takes everything so lightly and with little concern. At 12:30 PM my niece Susanna Martens went on to her eternal rest after a long illness. You have finished the battle and your Redeemer lives.

January 25

In Chortitza elder Jacob Dyck preached the preparatory sermon. Jacob Dyck preached in Neuendorf, D. Wiens in Osterwick, Jacob Regier in Burwalde. Prepare us as worthy guests for your table.

January 27

Today my niece Susanna Martens was buried. Reverend Johann Penner preached the funeral sermon. She was sixty-two years old and had given birth to three children. One daughter is still alive. Rest in peace.

January 3

Saturday. After a nineteen-day illness I made my first excursion to Schoenhorst for the engagement of Catarina [Rempel] to Abraham Friesen. Thank you, my Saviour, for restoring my health.

February 1

Elder Jacob Dyck celebrated holy communion in Chortitza with three hundred and thirty members. Jacob Regier preached the preparatory sermon in Neuendorf.

February 8

I preached the sermon of thanksgiving in Chortitza on Ephesians 1:3. In Neuendorf elder Jacob Dyck celebrated holy communion with two hundred and fifty-five members. Be with us all Lord Jesus. Amen.

During the afternoon I presided at the marriage of Elisabeth Lepp and David Rempel, the son of my sister, Mrs. D. Rempel of Schoenhorst. [The ceremony] was held locally at the Peter Lepp residence. The Lord's blessing rest upon this couple.

February 15

I preached the sermon of thanksgiving in Neuendorf on Ephesians 1:3, H. Penner did so in Osterwick. The other H. Penner preached in Chortitza. Praise and thanks to you my Saviour for all your love.

During the afternoon I presided at the marriage of Catarina, the daughter of my brother-in-law Dirk Rempel of Schoenhorst, and Abraham Friesen from Osterwick. The Lord's blessing rest upon this couple.

February 19

Jacob F. of Osterwick appeared before the *Kirchenkonvent*. He had obtained eggs to sell from Sch?, which was contrary to regulations. Fast and Siemens had a dispute about a rental agreement. Fast was unhappy with it and had given the matter over to the district office. The office advised Siemens to reconcile with Fast, which he refused to do. He was given until Sunday to make his peace with Fast and apologize to the district office. If this did not occur the matter would be placed before the congregation for judgement. Covetousness is the root of all evil.

February 22

Elder Jacob Dyck preached in Chortitza on Hebrews 12:12. Johann Dyck preached in Neuendorf, H. Penner in Osterwick. O Lord Jesus, grant us the strength to live acceptable lives before you.

Bruederschaft. Since Abraham Penner from the *chutor* continues to carry on with a Russian girl and has made her pregnant, he was excommunicated from the congregation. The Lord have mercy on him.

Note: On February 19 at 3 PM Martin Dyck of Einlage, who had been drinking liquor for some time, fell off the wagon in a drunken state and was instantly killed. He was on his way to Yekaterinoslav.

February 24

I preached the funeral sermon on ? for Martin Dyck of Einlage at the home of Cornelius Epp. He reached the age of fifty-three years, three months, two days and eleven hours. He was married for some twenty-eight years and sired six children, all of whom are alive. He had twelve grandchildren, two of whom died. His death is a warning to all of us.

February 26

On Thursday the widow Mrs. Abraham Neufeld and her son Abraham appeared before the *Kirchenkonvent*. There were rumours they were carrying on, but since there was no direct evidence they were admonished and departed in peace. . . .

March 1

Elder Jacob Dyck preached in Chortitza on Matthew 26:26-46. Johann Dyck preached in Neuendorf, H. Penner in Osterwick. Let me be always concious of your suffering and pain.

March 2

I and Jacob Epp and the two ? travelled to the sheep farm.

March 3

I preached on the *chutor* of Cornelius Rempel in the home of Sawatzky. I also preached the funeral sermon on Rom. 6:13 for the newborn Abraham Sawatzky who only lived one hour. Rest in peace little angel.

March 7

We travelled on very muddy roads but arrived home safely in the evening. Thanks to the Lord. Pastor ? of Prischib and ? from the Crimea just arrived.

March 8

They left for Yekaterinoslav in the afternoon.

March 15
H. Penner preached in Chortitza on Matthew 26:36-38. Elder J. Dyck preached in Neuendorf, Johann Dyck in Osterwick.

March 18
I preached the funeral sermon on ? for our member, sister Catarina Gronau from Burwalde (she belonged to the Kronsweide congregation). She died on March 15 at 10 PM after an illness of four days. She reached the age of fifty-two years. She was married for twenty-four years and gave birth to eight children, four of whom died. She had six grandchildren, one of whom died.

March 21
Our children, the Jacob Epps, moved to the community sheep farm on land belonging to ? . It is fifty verst from here. The Lord go with them and bless their endeavours.

March 22
I preached in Chortitza on Luke 22:39-44. H. Penner preached in Neuendorf, elder Jacob Dyck in Osterwick.

March 27
I preached the funeral sermon on Hebrews 12:14 for our member brother Peter ? in the home of the deceased in Einlage. He died on March 23 at 10 PM following a three-week illness. He reached the age of eighty-one years and one month. He was married for fifty-six years, two months and six days. He sired six children, one of whom died. He had twenty grandchildren, four of whom died. Rest in peace, dear brother.

March 29
I preached in Chortitza on Isaiah 53:7. H. Penner preached in Neuendorf, J. Dyck in Osterwick, Johann Penner in Rosengart, J. Regier in Nieder Chortitza. I want to be yours, dear Lord, forever.

April 5
I preached in Neuendorf on Isaiah 53:4. Johann Penner preached in Chortitza, H. Penner in Osterwick, elder Jacob Dyck in Burwalde.

Thank you, my Lord, for your great love which led you to die [for us].

April 12

Palm Sunday. I preached in Neuendorf on Matthew 21:1-9. Johann Penner preached in Chortitza, H. Penner in Osterwick.

April 15

H. Dyck Sn. from Nieder Chortitza and his brother-in-law Peter Rempel appeared before the *Kirchenkonvent* because of a quarrel. They were reconciled. Gerhard Siemens and Abraham Hiebert from Chortitza and Abraham Giesbrecht from Rosenthal also appeared. Siemens was charged with drinking strong liquor. Giesbrecht had brought liquor to Siemen's home, which he [Siemens] acknowledged but Giesbrecht denied. He claimed he only did it once. Siemens said it was more than once. Hiebert denied everything. Nothing was resolved though they promised to stop drinking. Such incidents are on the increase in our congregation and discipline is on the decline. Lord have mercy on us.

April 17

Good Friday. J. Regier preached in Chortitza on Isaiah 53:8-10. J. Penner preached in Neuendorf, D. Wiens in Osterwick. O Lord Jesus, let me always remember your suffering and pain.

In the afternoon I preached the funeral sermon for the adopted daughter of Cornelius Hiebert at the Einlage community farm. Her name was Maria Funk. She died on April 15, 12:30 AM after an illness of three weeks and five days and reached the age of eight years, seven months, and two days. In her innocence she went to be with the Lord.

April 18

I preached the funeral sermon for our member sister Agata Reimer of Einlage. She delivered healthy male twins on the morning of April 14. She reached the age of forty-four years and was married for twenty-four years. She gave birth to thirteen children, three of whom died. Rest in peace, dear sister.

April 19

The first day of Easter. I preached in Osterwick on Mark 16:1-8. Elder Jacob Dyck used the same text in Chortitza. Johann Penner preached in Neuendorf, Johann Dyck in Einlage, H. Penner in Burwalde, J. Dyck in Nieder Chortitza, D. Wiens in Einlage, J. Regier in Rosengart. "If Christ has not been raised, our preaching is useless and so is your faith" [1 Cor. 15:14]. Christ has truly risen.

April 20

The second day of Easter. I preached in Chortitza on Luke 24:13-35. J. Dyck preached in Neuendorf, Johann Penner in Osterwick.

April 21

This afternoon my brother-in-law H. Friesen and his wife and my brother-in-law Warkentin passsed through. They have children on the community farm.

April 23

After the H. Thiessens, their sons Heinrich and Peter and daughter Margareta had visited us and their other friends here, they left this morning for their return journey.

April 26

I presented the articles of faith [in Chortitza] using the text Romans 10:10. J. Regier did so in Neuendorf, J. D. in Osterwick. H. Penner preached in Nieder Chortitza. Jesus, strengthen our faith. I notified elder Jacob Dyck about a rumour that Mrs. Gerhard ? had given birth and had ?. The witnesses were Peter H. and D. Dyck. I recommended that the matter be investigated.

April 28

Abraham Zacharias and Abraham Friesen from Osterwick were ordered to appear [before the *Kirchenkonvent*] because of a report of elder J. Braun of Bergthal. According to [the widow] P. Dyck, they both had an affair with her before she was married. Zacharias admitted it. Friesen did not. The Lord will bring to light what is hidden in darkness.

May 3

Elder J. Dyck presented the articles of faith in Chortitza. I did the same in Neuendorf, J. Regier did so in Osterwick. I believe, Lord help my unbelief.

Bruederschaft in Chortitza. Zacharias was excommunicated as was the widow P. Dyck, who committed adultery with Gerhard Friesen. Lord, have mercy on us.

At 2 PM the head of the colonies, privy councillor [von] Hahn arrived in Chortitza. His excellency stayed with Schwarz. They walked incognito through the entire village. In the afternoon they inspected the colony plantation, the district offices, the church and the school. Accompanied by district officials, he visited Burwalde, Nieder Chortitza, Schoenberg. For lunch they were at the community sheep farm in Bergthal. Then it was on to Osterwick, Rosenthal and Schoenfeld.[1]

May 5

They visited Schoenhorst, Neuhorst, Neuenburg, Neuendorf, Neu-Kronsweide and Alt-Kronsweide. Satisfied with their visit they left for ? at 5 PM. May the angel of the Lord be their guide.

May 8

The privy councillor's party left for the Molotschna via Einlage.

May 10

I presented the articles of faith in Neuendorf. Elder Jacob Dyck did so in Chortitza. In Neuendorf there were thirteen male and twelve female candidates. In Chortitza there were seventy-six in all. Ignite, O Lord Jesus, the flame of faith in all of us.

In the afternoon the minister Mathies from Rudnerweide was with us for a one-and-a-half-hour visit.

Elder Jacob Dyck readmitted Abraham Zacharias and the widow P. Dyck as members of the congregation.

May 17

I presented articles one to nine in Neuendorf. Elder Jacob Dyck presented them in Chortitza. The baptismal candidates were listed for the second time: eighty-five in Chortitza, thirty in Neuendorf. The Lord's will be done.

May 24

I presented articles eight to the end in Neuendorf while elder Jacob

Dyck did so in Chortitza. The baptismal candidates were presented for the third time. There were the same number as mentioned above. May their names be written in heaven. Gerhard Friesen was readmitted to the congregation by elder Jacob Dyck. The Lord be merciful to him.

May 26

On Tuesday elder Jacob Dyck catechized eighty-five baptismal candidates in the Chortitza church. May the dear Saviour bless the care given to these young plants.

Elder Jacob Dyck received a letter from elder Bernhard Fast in Halbstadt which contained a copy of a letter to Fast from Johann Cornies in Ohrloff. It instructs elder Jacob Dyck on direct orders from his excellency, the privy councillor von Hahn, to cease all involvement in ecclesiastical matters [in the Molotschna]. If unrest continues in Warkentin's congregation, the instigator will be reported to the privy councillor. Warkentin would then be imprisoned [in Verwahrung] in Orechow. Peace nourishes, conflict destroys.

May 28

Ascension Day. Elder Jacob Dyck preached in Chortitza on the theme: Our walk is in heaven. He catechized eighty-five candidates for the second time. I preached in Neuendorf on Mark 16:50-53. I catechized the thirty candidates here for the first time.

May 29

I preached the funeral sermon on the Gruenfeld community sheep farm at the home of the sheepmaster George Schmit. His daughter Anna died of the measles on May 28 at 8 AM. She was nine years, six months and two days old. Jesus accepts the children.

May 30

I preached the funeral sermon for the young man Abraham Schroeder in Einlage. He died on May 27 at 7:30 PM after an illness of eight days and eight hours. He reached the age of twenty-one years and three months. Rest in peace.

May 31

I catechized the baptismal candidates in Neuendorf for the second time. In Chortitza elder Jacob Dyck addressed the customary questions to the baptismal candidates. May grace be with us all.

June 1

I and our two sons David and Jacob began our journey to the wool market in Charkov. We arrived there safely on the evening of June 8. The wool buyers arrived at noon on June 8. They were four days late. I sold our wool at twenty-one rubles per *pud* for the washed wool, thirteen rubles for the unwashed wool. We left Charkov at noon on June 11 and arrived at my brother-in-law H. Thiessen's at noon on June 12. On Sunday, June 14, we arrived home safe and sound. Eternal thanks to God for his gracious protection and provision.

Note: There was ample wool at the wool market. There were a lot of buyers, but too many sellers. About sixty thousand *pud* were put in warehouses and some fifteen thousand *pud* was still unsold at the market on June 13.

At the onset of the market the hightest price for the washed wool reached twenty-five rubles, unwashed seventeen rubles. Towards the end of the market the washed sold at seventeen rubles, the unwashed thirteen. Until the Preschogino station the grain crop looked poor, towards Constantinograd average. It steadily improved as we passed Constantinograd, and was excellent some fifteen *verst* away. The haycrops followed the same pattern.

Oats sold from one ruble thirty kopecks per *Mirke* to one ruble eighty kopecks. Hay sold from sixty to eighty kopecks per load. Rye flour from two rubles to two rubles and twenty-five kopecks per *pud*.

June 7

On the first day of Pentecost elder Jacob Dyck preached in Chortitza. O Lord Jesus, pour out Your Spirit of grace and of prayer on all.

June 8

Elder Jacob Dyck baptized the candidates in Chortitza. In Neuendorf the articles of faith were presented. The baptismal candidates sat on the front benches and H. Penner asked them the required questions. May the Holy Jesus crown all with His blessing.

June 14
Elder Jacob Dyck baptized the candidates in Neuendorf. H. Penner preached the preparatory sermon in Chortitza. Prepare us all, O Holy Jesus, for holy communion.

June 21
Elder Jacob Dyck celebrated holy communion with three hundred and sixteen members of the Chortitza congregation. I too was a poor guest at the table You prepared, O Lord, and which refreshed our hearts. Brother J. Regier preached the preparatory sermon in Neuendorf. Create in us, O God, a pure heart.

June 28
Elder Jacob Dyck celebrated holy communion in Neuendorf with four hundred and forty-one members of the congregation. "Give thanks to the Lord, for he is good; his love endures forever." [Psa. 107:1]

July 2
Thursday. Aron Peters and Gerhard Siemens appeared before the *Kirchenkonvent*. Both had imbibed liquor at the annual fair in Michailow. On their return trip they travelled on the same coach as the consul general from Odessa. He had complained [about their behaviour] to the district head Johann Siemens. They apologized and rather regretted their actions. The congregation will decide what to do with them on Sunday. O poisonous liquor, what destruction you bring.

Elder Jacob Dyck showed us a letter from privy councillor von Hahn. The elder earlier inquired about the duty-free importation of hymn books from Prussia. His excellency demanded the title of the hymn book and a title list of the songs it contained. This material was to be sent to the *Comitaet*. Elder Jacob Dyck informed us that a response was forthcoming and that they wanted five hundred hymnals. I had not heard of this before.

July 5
Jacob Dyck preached in Chortitza on 1 Corinthians 15:1-2. David Wiens preached the sermon of thanksgiving in Neuendorf, H. Penner in Neu-Osterwick.

Bruederschaft. Gerhard Siemens did not admit to drinking liquor, and asked for tolerance. He was forgiven. Aron Peters acted similarly. Since there were no eyewitnesses to the events of July 2 the matter was given over to the district office. Everyone tries to minimize their failures and transgressions. Can we continue this way?

D. Niebuhr from ? and Maria Penner from Nieder Chortitza were accepted as members of the congregation by elder Jacob Dyck. God be merciful to us sinners.

July 12

[In Chortitza] brother J. Dyck preached on 1 Corinthians 15:1-2. David Wiens preached in Neuendorf. H. Penner in Osterwick, J. Regier in Nieder Chortitza, J. Penner in Rosengart. Bless these messages, O Lord Jesus.

Bruederschaft. Thiessen's wife from Rosenthal was accepted as a member of the congregation by elder Jacob Dyck. May her apparent repentance be genuine. The following charges were brought against Abraham Hiebert of Chortitza: he changed the identification of a lamb belonging to the farmer B. Rempel by sheering off the wool containing the identification mark; he took two more *Mirke* of rye, which should have gone to Abraham Kopp, from the school teacher Johann Wieler; on behalf of children he had sold one hundred and forty pud of rye flour to a Russian in Tamakovka but kept two rubles and sixty-two kopecks for himself. There were other things as well. He gave a number of excuses which were not accepted and he was excommunicated from the congregation. The Lord have mercy on him.

July 14

The newly elected elders from the Molotschna, Heinrich Wiens and ? visited elder Jacob Dyck. I don't know why.

July 16

The members of the *Waisenamt*, Dyck, Aron Thiessen and Peter Wieler from Nieder Chortitza met with the *Kirchenkonvent*. Wieler, who was the guardian of the deceased Loepky's children, wish to be relieved of his responsibility. He absolutely insisted upon this. The matter will be decided by the brethren on Sunday.

W. Hildebrand and Morgenstern (?) from Einlage were present because of a dispute. It was discussed and they were reconciled. All is vanity, "The world and its desires pass away but the man who does the will of God lives forever." [I John 2:17].

July 19

H. Penner preached in Chortitza on Psalm 119:33. J. D. preached in Neuendorf, D. Wiens in Osterwick.

Bruederschaft. The guardianship of Peter Wieler in Nieder Chortitza was discussed. He did not want to accept it. It was left to his conscience so nothing was really resolved.

July 22

In the afternoon Mr. John Melville, agent of the British Bible Society, arrived at my house. From here he left for Einlage. I accepted six boxes of Bibles and New Testaments from him for sale and distribution.

Note: On June 22 at 4 PM a storm emerged which developed into a hurricane. A cloudburst occurred in Schoenhorst, Neuendorf, and Neuenburg with hail the size of grapes and chicken eggs. In Chortitza a few roofs were wrecked and some trees broken or uprooted. In Neuenburg a windmill and two houses were destroyed and three houses lost their roof joists. Some houses in Neuendorf and Schoenhorst were flooded by one-half to three feet of water. Fences, implements, hay stacks and grain were swept away. The floods drowned sheep, cattle, dogs and poultry. A sheep barn in Neuendorf could not withstand the force of the water. It collapsed, killing or drowning the sheep. The community sheep barn in Schoenfeld was completely destroyed and the sheep killed or injured. The shepherdess was killed by a piece of wood when the barn collapsed. The Russian villages of Michailovka and especially Tomakovka were especially hard hit. More than ten people died in the floods. A serious message from the Lord.

July 25

I preached the funeral sermon for the newborn Jacob Epp, son of our member brother C. Epp in Rosengart. He died after a nine-day illness on July 24, 1 AM at the age of thirty nine weeks. J. Melville arrived at our house in the evening.

July 26

H. Penner preached in Chortitza, Jacob D. in Neuendorf, D. Wiens in Osterwick, Johann Penner in Burwalde.

Bruederschaft. Abraham Hiebert was forgiven after he apologized to all he had wronged and admitted his guilt. He was readmitted into the congregation by elder Jacob Dyck.

After J. Melville had listened to the sermon and had lunch with us he left for Einlage. Tomorrow he continues his journey to the Molotschna. The Lord's angel go with him.

July 29

I and my wife and four children left for the sheep farm where we found our children well and happy. What a contrast—we are arid and dry, there everything is a vibrant green. Thank you, my Saviour, for everything.

August 2

Jacob Dyck preached in Chortitza, H. Penner in Neuendorf, J. Dyck in Neu-Osterwick, D. Wiens in Nieder Chortitza.

August 3

We returned from the sheep farm safe and sound. Thank the Lord for his gracious protection.

August 15

I preached the funeral sermon on ? for our departed member Gerhard Martens at the home of the deceased in Neuenburg. He died on August 13 at 9:30 AM of a stroke, after suffering for eight days. He reached the age of forty-four years, ten months and eleven days. He was married for nineteen years and sired eight children, one of whom died. Rest in peace until the blessed and joyous resurrection.

August 16

Elder Jacob Dyck preached in Chortitza, Johann D. in Neuendorf, H. Penner in Osterwick.

August 22

I preached the funeral sermon on Psalm 90 for our member, sister

Helena Wall, in the home of the deceased in Neuhorst. She died on August 20 at 6:15 PM of a stroke, after a twelve-day illness. She reached the age of forty-three years, seven months, three weeks and four days. She was married for twenty-five years and gave birth to eleven children, of whom four died. She had one grandchild, who is alive.

August 23

Elder Jacob Dyck preached [in Chortitza], Johann D. in Neuendorf, H. Penner in Osterwick, J. Penner in Burwalde. Walk happily and seemly in the laws of the Lord.

Bruederschaft. Gerhard Penner from Schoenhorst was excommunicated from the congregation because of his drinking. May the Lord enlighten him.

August 26

Elder H. Wiens and his brother arrived from the Molotschna to visit elder Jacob Dyck.

August 27

The two returned. Why did they come? The Lord be with them.

August 30

I preached in Chortitza. Jacob Regier in Neuendorf. Johann Dyck in Osterwick.

Bruederschaft. Gerhard Penner was readmitted into the congregation by elder Jacob Dyck. The Lord enlighten him.

September 5

At 12:30 AM our daughter-in-law, Mrs. Dirk Epp gave birth to a healthy daughter. She was called Helena. Our daughter-in-law stayed with us until her delivery. Praise and thanks to You, my Saviour, for Your goodness and faithfulness. Let this little one grow up to Your glory and give joy to her parents and grandparents. Johann Friesen, his wife and two children from Blumenort stopped by for lunch.

September 6

In the morning they left for the sheep farm with our son David in order to visit the Bernd Friesens. I preached in Chortitza on Ephesians

3: 18-19, H. Penner Sr. preached in Neuendorf, J.P. in Osterwick, H. Penner Jr. in Nieder Chortitza.

September 11

After the Johann Friesens from Blumenort visited their friends, they left for home today.

September 12

I preached the funeral sermon for Catarina Dyck, the daughter of Dirk Dyck. She died on Saturday at 3 AM following a fever of eight weeks. At the end she developed dropsy. She reached the age of fifteen years and twenty-seven days. She was broken like a flower which blossomed early in the morning but was cut down before noon and fades away.

September 13

I preached in Neuendorf on Ephesians 3: 18,19. H. Penner Jr. preached in Chortitza. "Blessed is the man who does not walk in the counsel of the wicked." [Psa. 1:1]

September 14

I and our children, the D. Epps, left for their home on their sheep farm.

September 18

I and the Jacob Epps returned. Praise and thanks to God.

September 20

I preached in Neuendorf on Luke 19:10. H. Penner Sr. preached in Chortitza, D. Wiens in Osterwick, Jakob Dyck in Burwalde, Johann Penner in Rosengart. "For the Son of Man came to seek..." [Luke 19:10].

September 23

Bruederschaft in Chortitza. The widow Harder nee Vogt was excommunicated from the congregation. While a widow she had committed adultery with Gerhard Friesen. Abraham Teigroew from Osterwick also appeared. In spring he had stolen a sack of wheat from Jacob Harder. His wife, troubled by the theft, reported him and he admitted it. The youth Thiessen, who was baptized in the spring of this year and worked for D. Redekop, had stolen a chest containing sixty rubles from the widow Reimer (a Lutheran) during the night. The Lord have mercy on them all.

This afternoon our children the Jacob Epps together with their parents-in-law, the Peter Klassens, left for Mariupol to visit their friends. I and my wife visited our children in Schoenhorst. Mrs. Rempel gave birth to a healthy son Diderich on September 14. Mother and child were doing fine. Thanks to the Lord Jesus for all His love and benefits.

September 24

Jacob Wieler of Chortitza and Heinrich Wiebe of Kronsweide appeared before the *Lehrdienst*. Both had refused to pay the dues levied by the church. Both promised to pay and were dismissed. What has happened to our community spirit? It has disappeared from the congregation.

September 27

Elder Jacob Braun of Bergthal preached in Osterwick on Matthew 3: 8-10. Johann Penner preached in Chortitza, H. Penner Sr. in Nieder Chortitza, Johann Dyck in Neuendorf. Give us the strength for true repentance.

On Thursday Peter Driedger from Neuendorf, Schreiber and Gerhard Penner from Chortitza appeared before the *Lehrdienst* because of their heavy drinking. They promised to improve and were dismissed. We condone a dead morality devoid of spirit and life.

October?

I preached the funeral sermon for our deceased member, sister Helena Dyck from the *Kamp*.[2] She died on October 2, at 5 PM after a ten-day illness. She reached the age of sixty-two years and two months. Her first marriage lasted twenty-four years. She gave birth to nine children, four of whom died. She had seventeen grandchildren, seven of whom died. Her second marriage lasted fourteen years. There were no children. Rest in peace, dear sister, until the end of days.

October 3

I preached the funeral sermon for little Aron, the son of Aron Ens in Schoenhorst. He had accidentally stabbed himself in the abdomen so that his bowels were exposed. He died after twenty-four hours, at 1 AM. He was seven years, one month and five days old. The Lord's ways are mysterious.

October 4

I preached the thanksgiving sermon in Osterwick on Acts 14:17. Elder J. Brown from Bergthal preached in Neuendorf, Johann Penner in Chortitza. Praise and thanks to you, my dear Saviour, for all your benefits.

Bruederschaft. Abraham Teigroew from Kronsthal was readmitted to the church by elder Jacob Dyck.

October 5

Elder J. Braun and his family left for home. The Lord accompany him.

October 7

The teacher Peter Epp and his wife from Heubuden [Prussia] arrived at our neighbour, C. Epp.

October 10

The teacher P. Epp continued his journey to ? On Monday they will resume their journey. J. Regier preached in Chortitza, Johann Penner in Neuendorf, H. Penner Sr. in Osterwick. Brother J. Regier presided over the marriage of Dirk Thiessen and Catarina Thiessen in the church.

Bruederschaft. The youth H. Thiessen from Neuendorf was readmitted into the congregation by elder Jacob Dyck. The Lord give him strength to avoid the tyranny of sin.

October 11

I preached the funeral sermon on ? for our deceased member, sister Anganeta Sawatzky (my wife's niece) in the school house at ?. She died on October 9 at 4 PM after an illness of ten days. She reached the age of forty-two years, two months and twenty-seven days. She was married for twenty-one years, ten months and eight days and gave birth to seven children, four of whom died. Jesus will grant her eternal joy after much suffering.

October 12
I and my dear wife and Tienchen travelled to the sheep farm. We returned safe and sound.

October 18
Brother Jacob Regier preached in Chortitza, Johann Penner in Neuendorf, H. Penner Sr. in Osterwick. H. Penner Jr. preached for me in Burwalde. Bless these messages, Lord Jesus.

October 25
D. Wiens preached in Chortitza on Acts 10:43. Johann Dyck preached in Neuendorf. In the afternoon Bernd Fast, his brother-in-law Dyck and his wife left here after visiting their friends.

November 1
David Wiens preached in Chortitza, J. Regier in Neuendorf, J. Penner in Osterwick. The Lord bless the messages.

November 3
I preached the funeral sermon on Psalm 36:3-6 for our neighbour, the deceased member sister Catarina Dyck. She died on October 29 at 3 PM following a ten-day illness. She reached the age of forty-seven years, nine months and twenty-one days. She was married for some twenty-seven years and four months. She gave birth to eight children, of whom two died. She had two grandchildren, both of whom are alive. Rest in peace.

November 8
Jacob Dyck preached in Chortitza, D. Wiens in Neuendorf, H. Penner in Osterwick. Christ is all in all.

November 12
I presided at the marriage of the Johann Schellenberg and Anne Wiebe on Chortitza Island at the residence of Jacob Wiebe. Holy Jesus spread your grace over this couple.

November 15
I preached in Burwalde on Luke 19:10. Jacob Dyck preached in

Chortitza, H. Penner in Osterwick, D. Wiens in Neuendorf, Johann Penner in Rosengart. Jesus accepts sinners, of whom I am chief.

November 22

Brother H. Penner Jr. preached in Chortitza, D. Wiens in Neuendorf. Christ is the end of the law.

November 29

First Sunday of advent. H. Penner Jr. preached in Chortitza, J. Dyck in Neuendorf, D. Wiens in Osterwick.

December 6

Second Sunday of advent. Johann Dyck preached in Chortitza, H. Penner Jr. in Neuendorf, D. Wiens in Osterwick.

December 10

Lehrdienst. The Chortitza mayor Cornelius von Bergen and the pub owner Absalom Bartsch got into a dispute. They were reconciled and left in peace. The love of God and love of the brother is becoming scarcer.

December 13

Third Sunday of advent. Johann Dyck preached in Chortitza on John 1:1-13. H. Penner Jr. preached in Neuendorf, Jacob Dyck in Osterwick. Let Your light dawn in all of us.

Brother D. Penner talked about the inspection of the village schools. I want to show more interest in this than I have until now. I asked elder Jacob Dyck to take the initiative.

December 20

Fourth Sunday of advent. Elder Jacob Dyck preached on Luke 21. Johann Dyck Jr. preached in Neuendorf, H. Penner Jr. in Osterwick, D. Wiens in Burwalde. The Lord's blessing rest upon these messages.

December 25

Elder J. Dyck preached on Luke 2:1-11. Johann Dyck Jr. in Neuendorf, H. Penner Jr. in Osterwick, Johann Penner in Burwalde. O my Saviour be born anew in all of us.

December 26

I preached in Chortitza on John 1:14. Elder Jacob Dyck preached in Neuendorf, Johann Dyck in Osterwick. Lord Jesus "stay with us for it is nearly evening..." [Luke 24:29].

December 27

On this last Sunday of the year, I preached in Chortitza on Eph. 4:22. Elder Jacob Dyck preached in Neuendorf, H. Penner in Osterwick. Lord Jesus, forgive us all our sin which we knowingly and unknowingly committed during the past year.

The beginning of this year was moist, then it became very dry. The late summer and fall were moist. There was a lot of illness in the community, especially colds and head aches.

One hundred and fifty-seven males and one hundred and fifteen females were born this past year. Fifty-nine males and fifty-seven females died. There were one hundred and fifty-six more births than deaths. Sixty-six couples were married.

The early crops scarcely returned the seed. Millet produced well. The later grains were average. Rye seeded into summer fallow did well, the rye seeded into stubble poorly. Vegetables were average. There was no fruit. In fall and winter there was rain, but little snow. The lowest temperature was minus 14. Hay was in short supply and demanded a high price in fall. An average load cost between twenty and thirty-five rubles. It was somewhat higher at the beginning of winter.

A *chetverik* of wheat sold for sixteen rubles, rye twelve rubles, barley eight rubles, oats six rubles, millet six rubles. Butter sold for twenty to twenty-eight kopecks per pound.

Congregational life is in a sad state—drunkenness, adultery, fornication, lies and gossip are the order of the day.

The economy is doing well. The privy councillor von Hahn, the chairman of the *Comitaet*, is getting things moving which earlier were not thought possible.

The *Zentralschule* opened in summer and is operational. The teacher is H. Heese. Six children are being trained as school teachers. The school has thirty-two children.

Tree plantations of half a dessiatine per farmer have been ordered and village plans for the same formulated.

Elder Jacob Warkentin of Altonau has been stripped of his office by privy councillor von Hahn because of disorder in his congregation and other disputes. The privy councillor ordered four new elders be elected. All this only intensified the division. May the Lord Jesus protect us from such a split.

Rumour has it we too face a crisis—a difficult time for elder J. Dyck. May God direct all things to our good for the sake of his eternal love. Amen.

Due to the unrest in the Molotschna, the farmer Thun was expelled on orders from state councillor von Hahn. Almost eighty farmers had to spend several days doing penal work.

Endnotes

[1]Eugenii von Hahn owed his eventual appointment as head of the *Comitaet* to the Grand Duchess Elena Pavlovna who visited the Chortitza in 1841. Initially he was appointed as a deputy to Ivan N. Inzov. When Inzov was incapacitated by a stroke and died, Hahn became chairperson. Epp praises his ability to get things done, though he is not impressed by his ruthlessness when it came to interference in church affairs. Von Hahn promoted agricultural innovation, schools and school attendance, industrial development, village order and efficient administration.

[2] The term *Kamp* was frequently used to designate the Island of Chortitza.

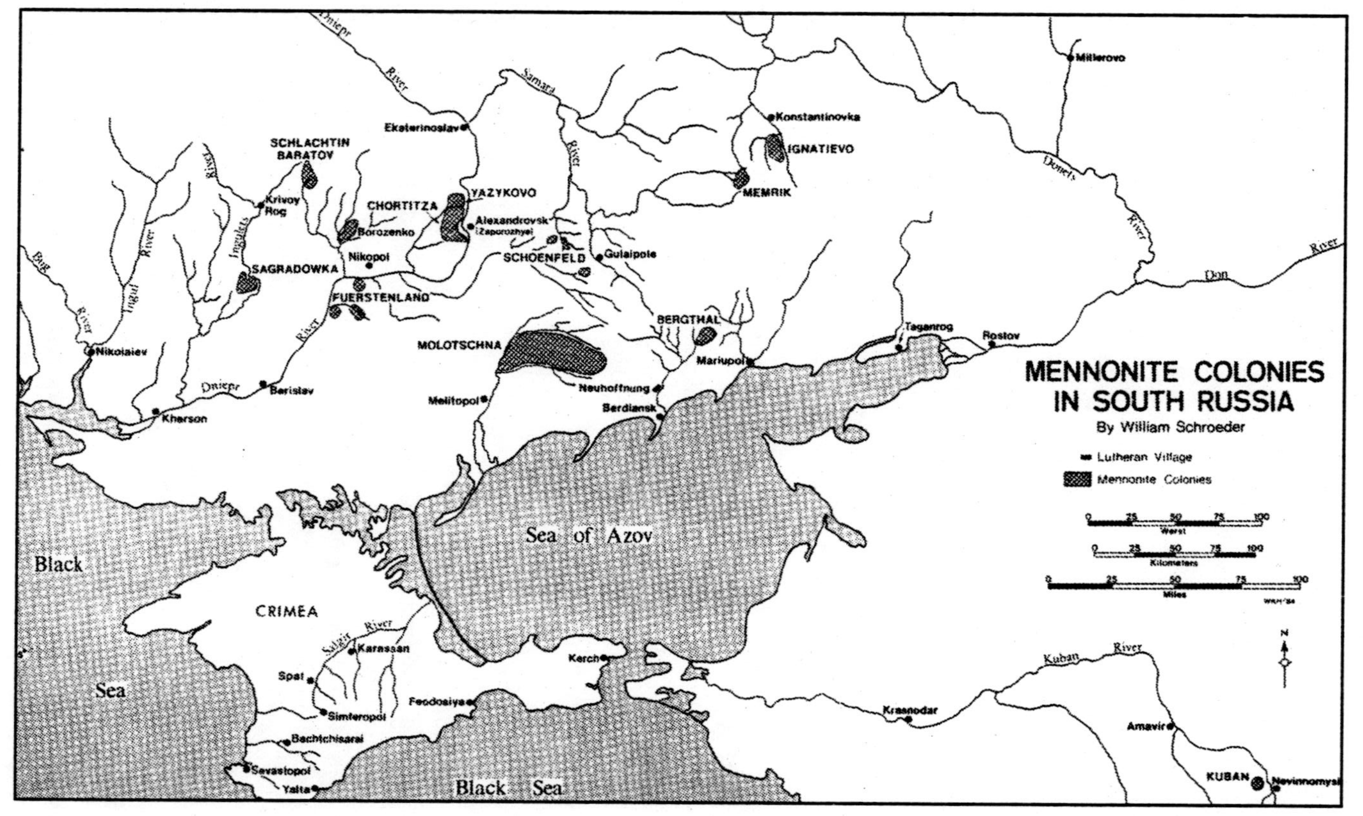
MENNONITE COLONIES
IN SOUTH RUSSIA
By William Schroeder
Lutheran Village
Mennonite Colonies
Werst
Kilometers
Miles
N
SCHLACHTIN
BARATOV
CHORTITZA
YAZYKOVO
SAGRADOWKA
FUERSTENLAND
SCHOENFELD
MOLOTSCHNA
BERGTHAL
MEMRIK
IGNATIEVO
KUBAN
CRIMEA
Sea of Azov
Black Sea
Black
Sea
Millerovo
Konstantinovka
Ekaterinoslav
Krivoy Rog
Borozenko
Nikopol
Alexandrovsk (Zaporozhye)
Gulaipole
Nikolaiev
Berislav
Kherson
Melitopol
Neuhoffnung
Berdiansk
Mariupol
Taganrog
Rostov
Karassan
Spat
Simferopol
Feodosiya
Kerch
Bachtchisarai
Sevastopol
Yalta
Krasnodar
Amavir
Nevinnomysk
Dniepr River
Samara River
Bug River
Ingul River
Ingulets River
Donets River
Don River
Kuban River
Salgir River

1843

January 1

"Commit your way to the Lord; trust in him and he will do this." [Psa. 37:5]

On Friday, New Year's Day, I preached in Neuendorf on Ephesians 4: 22-24. H. Penner Senior preached in Chortitza, D.J. in Osterwick, Johann Penner in Einlage, D. Wiens in Schoenberg. In Your grace give us new life and new salvation.

January 3

H. Penner Senior preached in Chortitza, H. Penner Junior in Neuendorf, D. Wiens in Osterwick, J.D. in Nieder Chortitza. "Create in me a pure heart, O God, and renew a steadfast spirit within me." [Psa. 51:10]

In the afternoon our children Jacob Epp and his wife, who had arrived on December 23, left.

January 5

This morning Dirk Epp and his wife, who arrived here on December 31, returned to the sheep farm.

January 6

I preached in Osterwick on Matthew 2: 1-12. Brother Johann Penner preached in Chortitza, H. Penner Senior in Neuendorf. "Arise, shine, for your light has come..." [Isa. 60:1].

January 7

A ministerial meeting in the Chortitza church. H. Hildebrand, who had been appointed as the guardian for the mentally ill Aron Wiebe from Einlage, did not wish to accept the responsibility and in spite of much encouragement refused to do so. It was decided to initiate school inspections. Elder Jacob Dyck was to do so in Rosenthal, I in Chortitza, brother H. Penner Senior in Einlage and the Island of Chortitza, the brothers H. Penner Jr. and Johann Dyck in Schoenhorst, Neuhorst, Neuendorf and Neuenburg. The brothers Jacob Dyck and David Wiens would inspect [the schools] in Kronstadt, Osterwick, Nieder Chortitza, Burwalde and Rosengart. Shortcomings are to be identified and remedied, the school teachers encouraged in their work and the high German language introduced.

Ministerial elections are to be held after the [annual] celebration of holy communion. May the Lord Jesus bless these undertakings so that everything may resound to His praise and to the salvation of us all.

January 10

Johann Penner preached in Chortitza, H. Penner Senior in Neuendorf, D. Wiens in Osterwick, J. Dyck in Burwalde.

Bruederschaft. Maria Penner from Nieder Chortitza had confessed that she slept with the young men Mantler and Peters. Both denied it. The matter was left to their conscience. ? was excommunicated from the congregation. The Lord will bring to light what was hidden.

January 13

I preached the funeral sermon on ? for Cornelius, the young son of Peter Krahn of Schoenwiese. He died on January 16 at 9 AM at the age of six years, seven months, and twenty-six days. Jesus accepts the children.

January 17

Elder Jacob Dyck preached in Chortitza for brother D. Wiens. The Lord bless the message. I will no longer preach [outside of Chortitza].

January 19

I returned from Yekaterinoslav safe and sound. I left with Gerhard Krahn from Chortitza on January 15. The roads were very bad for two days.

January 21

My neighbour's farm was sold by the *Waisenamt* in public auction to J.T. of Burwalde for two thousand, eight hundred and forty-five rubles. Three years ago he paid four thousand and fifty rubles for it. Everything—cattle, wagons etc. was sold. How quickly things change in this world.

January 24

D. Wiens preached in Chortitza on Acts 24:25. Do not allow us to postpone our repentance, O Lord Jesus, but use our time wisely.

Bruederschaft. Maria Penner from Nieder Chortitza was readmitted into the congregation. May the dear Saviour give her much grace for the sake of His great love.

February 7

Elder Jacob Dyck celebrated holy communion in the Chortitza church with 300 members. Do not remember our sins, O Lord Jesus, and enable us to truly love and to walk in holiness.

February 21

Brother H. Penner Jr. preached the thanksgiving sermon in Chortitza. Similar sermons were preached in Neuendorf and Osterwick. A heart dedicated to God is a true offering of thanks, for Jesus lives in such a heart.

February 22

I preached the funeral sermon on ? for Catarina, the wife of Peter ? in Chortitza. She was ill for seven days and died on February 18, 6 AM. She reached the age of seventy-five years, four weeks and one day. She was married for fifty-two years and five months. She gave birth to ten children, three of whom died. She had fifty-four grandchildren and six great grandchildren. There were seventy descendents in all. Rest in peace.

February 25

I preached the funeral sermon on Job 14:1-7 for the infant Maria Reinke, the daughter of W. Reinke from Einlage. She died after a sixteen-day illness on February 20 at 11 PM at the age of nine months and twelve days. "Let the children come unto me" [Mark 10:14].

Kirchenkonvent. The carpenter Peter Neufeld of Einlage had driven by Kroeker's residence in Kronstadt, swore at him and attacked him. The matter was referred to the brethren on Sunday. The darkness increases.

February 28

I preached in Osterwick on Psalm 39:6. Help us, O Lord Jesus, to live our lives to Your glory and to our salvation. In the afternoon I preached the funeral sermon for our deceased member, brother Peter Friesen, who died of a stroke after a three-day illness on February 26, at 10 AM. He reached the age of sixty-seven years, six months, three weeks and two days. He was married for forty-two years and six weeks. He sired eleven children, six of whom died. He had twenty-six grandchildren, twelve of whom are alive. Be gracious to his poor soul for the sake of your eternal love. Amen.

H. Penner preached in Chortitza. The Lord's blessing rest upon the message.

March 2

I and my dear wife together with the J. Dycks travelled to Yekaterinoslav to my brother-in-law H. Thiessen, in order to attend the funeral of his youngest son Julius Thiessen.

March 3

I preached the funeral sermon. Julius died on February 27 at 4 PM. following an illness of nine days. He reached the age of six years, one day and seventeen hours.

March 6

We returned on bad roads and arrived home safe and sound at 7 PM.

March 7

Johann Dyck preached in Chortitza. The Lord is near to them that call upon him. In February the young man Jacob Penner, who has long been living a dissolute life, joined the Russian Orthodox Church in Yekaterinoslav. May it be a blessing to him.

March 14

Elder Jacob Dyck preached in Chortitza. In You, O Lord, is my trust.

March 16

I presided at the wedding of ? and Anganeta Neustaedter at the Einlage home of Johann Neustaedter. The Lord be with them.

March 21

Elder Jacob Dyck preached in Chortitza on Matthew 26: 36-46. Lord may your bitter suffering constantly encourage me to earnestly flee the desires of sin.

Bruederschaft. Upon his confession of adultery ? Schellenberg of Blumengart was excommunicated from the church. Grant him true repentance.

March 23

I presided at the wedding of the widow Fast and Johann Stoess in Einlage.

March 25

On Thursday Johann Neustaedter, P. Janz, Abraham Isaak and his brother-in-law Neufeld, all of Einlage, were called before the *Kirchenkonvent* because of a fight. Only Isaak appeared.

March 27

I learned that several days ago elder Jacob Dyck received a sealed letter from his excellency von Hahn, but I know nothing of its contents.

March 28

I preached in Chortitza on Isaiah 50:7. I believe, Lord help my unbelief.

Bruederschaft. Bernd Schellenberg was readmitted to the congregation by elder Jacob Dyck.

Some Observations on the Months of January, February and March. January and February were more like summer than winter. The fields turned green, flowers emerged, field mice and snakes were abundant as were all sorts of summer birds except the swallows and storks. There were two thunder showers. The temperature reached twelve degrees Reaumur. Many had seeded their spring crops, which began to germinate. In March we had twelve degrees of frost and many of the potatoes were frozen. The spring planting apparently did not suffer. During the last days of March there was a terrible storm which destroyed many roofs and collapsed weak buildings. The storm lasted for two days yet produced thunder showers and warm temperatures of up to seventeen degrees.

The unrest in the Molotschna continues; if anything it is intensifying. Counterfeit currency dated 1821 came into circulation. They are searching for the Russian counterfeiters.

God knows what will come of all of this. There is a lot of activity —the planting of gardens and forests as well as agricultural development.

Spiritually we have reached a new low, especially in our ecclesiastical leadership. In our discussions we are more concerned with the decrees of our superiors than the fundamentals of our faith. Breaches are rapidly opening up in the walls of Zion and it will require a tremendous effort to close them. If the Lord does not intervene we will become like Sodom and Gomorrah. The Lord has been humbling me, but He will lift me out of the dust. Praise and thanks to Him through all eternity.

April 4

I preached in Chortitza on Matthew 21: 1-9 (Palm Sunday). Lord come into my heart.

Bruederschaft. Mrs. Abraham Reimer in Schoeneberg beat the child of the village shepherd and afterwards his mother. She had to pay the shepherd's wife ten rubles and was excommunicated from the congregation. Grant her a genuine change of heart.

April 9

Good Friday. I preached in Neuendorf on John 19:28-30. H. Penner Senior preached in Chortitza. Jesus is my hope and my Saviour is alive.

April 11

I preached in Neuendorf on Mark 16:1-8. H. Penner Senior preached on the same text in Chortitza. You, O Saviour, arose from the dead on the third day. You have died for my sins and arose for my justification and my eternal life. Give me strength for true repentance and for a holy life and holy walk. Amen.

April 12

I preached in Osterwick on Luke 24:13-35, Johann Penner preached in Chortitza. Praise and thanks to you Saviour.

April 13

I and my dear wife travelled to our children on the *chutor*, seven verst beyond Tomakovka. We found our daughter-in-law very ill. She was very happy with our visit.

April 14

She seemed somewhat better. My wife stayed and I returned home.

April 15

Deacon and ministerial elections were held in the Chortitza church. Brother Jacob Dyck received sixty-seven votes, Gerhard Ens in Neuendorf sixty-three. Both were elected as deacons. Deacon Jacob Wiens of Kronsthal was elected as teacher [minister] with ninety votes. My Saviour endow these men with your wisdom and with a holy spirit of love that they may be true examples to the flock. ? of Schoeneberg was accepted as a member of the congregation by elder Jacob Dyck.

April 16

I travelled with the Jacob Epps to the D. Epps. She was still very ill but I think the fever has broken and she is recovering. The Lord is the right and best doctor.

April 17
I and the J. Epps returned.

April 18
I preached in Neuendorf on Romans 10:10. Elder Jacob Dyck preached in Chortitza. In Osterwick D. Wiens read the articles of faith. Lord Jesus, help my unbelief.

April 23
I preached in Neuendorf on Romans 10:10. Elder Jacob Dyck preached in Chortitza. In Osterwick D. Wiens read articles one to nine for the second time. Jacob Dyck preached in Nieder Chortitza. Faith, love and hope, these three [remain].

End of the Diaries.

Appendix

A Glossary of Terms used in the Diaries

Ältester — an elder or bishop who usually presided over the Lord's Supper and administered baptism.

Anwohner — a renter or village cottager who normally owned no farm land in the village. In some instances he could own his dwelling.

chetverik — a dry measure equal to one eighth of a chetvert. Occasionally called *merka* in the diaries.

chetvert — a dry measure equal to 5.95 bushels or 2.099 hectolitres.

chutor — farms or a farm, owned or leased, outside the village.

Comitaet — an abbreviated term for *Das Fuersorge Komitee fuer auslaendischen Kolonisten Sued-Russlands*. This Guardian's Committee was established to deal with difficulties confronting foreign settlers in New Russia.

Bruederschaft — an assembly of all the male members of a given congregation. It's decisions on matters of public morality and discipline was final.

Dankpredigt — a sermon of thanks and praise preached on the Sunday after communion.

dessiatine — a measure of land equal to 2.7 acres or 1.0925 hectares.

Ehrsame — a designation applied to ministers and elders. It implied respect, maturity and seniority.

Lehrer — a minister elected by the congregation. He usually served in a variety of roles—pastor, preacher, reconciler, disciplinarian.

Lehrdienst — a ministerial council whose jurisdiction included most civil infractions or even criminal ones.

Gebietsamt — an administrative district or *volost* containing a specified number of villages

Kirchenkonvent — a term occasionally used by Epp in place of *Lehrdienst*.

pud — a weight equivalent to 36.11 pounds or 16.38 kilograms. There were 40 *funt* (0.9 pounds or 0.41 kilograms) in a pud.

Privilegium — a document signed by Tsar Paul I which detailed the terms of Mennonite settlement in Russia.

verst — a distance measure equal to 0.633 miles or 1.065 kilometres.

Zentralschule — a school somewhat equivalent, though perhaps surpassing, a level of a junior high school in North America.

9 781573 831574